Shifting the Spiritual Atmosphere

30 Prayers ✳ 30 Days ✳ 30 Minutes

> Journal Included

Sharon Mullins

Warning! Praying these prayers have been known to release angelic activity—causing your spiritual atmosphere to shift, advancing the Kingdom of God, and leaving you marked for HIM forever.

Part I has been designed for individual use and includes journal space to respond to the Lord as He provokes each to love and good deeds through these prophetic prayers. **Part II** is the same prayers, written for a couple or a group.

All Prayers are designed to be prayed out loud in a bold and declarative manner.

Table of Contents

Part I

For the Individual

Part II

For the Couple/Group

❧ Dedication ❧

To my Lord and Savior,
for generously flowing these prayers through me
and trusting me with such a treasure.

To my wonderful husband, Peter H. Mullins,
who encouraged me as a woman, wife, mother,
and grandmother of prayer—declaring that
he never knew anyone that prayed more...

To my mother and hero, Marilyn,
who released
this spiritual prophetic heritage within me.

To Rick and Tina Watson,
for helping, encouraging, and
pastoring me—always.

To Wanda, Betty, and Emily,
some of my best friends in the world...
for never giving up on me
and being such an encouragement and blessing!

For all that have prayed with me and for me
over the years as I developed prayer in others and me.

To my mentoring group, From Called to Chosen,
for allowing me to mentor you with joy.

To the Mountain Movers Prayer Group,
a willing participant in every prayer I wrote
and encouraging me every step of the way.

To John Minix for helping me get to the finish line.

ஐ Introduction ଔ

This book is the second in a series of prophetic, shifting prayers. Once God ruined me by flowing prophetic prayers through me, I could never be satisfied with an ordinary prayer life. His will is that all hear the heart-beat of Heaven and allow that to be put into words that flow from each of us to the world.

Prayer is the backbone of my life and the foundation to any good thing that is birthed through my church (Coweta Community Church in Newnan, Georgia), family, and me. To hear from heaven is something I will never tire of. I want that for you too! I want you to get so caught up in what God is saying that He invades your spiritual atmosphere daily. As I type these prayers, His presence becomes so thick that many times, my hands become stuck to my keyboard; I'm overwhelmed by Him.

Don't get me wrong; I'm not complaining! I long for more of these times. If you pray these prayers, I know you do too.

Come with me on a thirty-day prayer journey and allow the heart of the Father to flow from these pages into your life. I don't know what He'll do for you. Every testimony I get is different! I know this: He will meet you and you will never be the same—for your good and His glory. In the process, you, your friends, loved ones and church will be encouraged, blessed, and wrecked for HIM. You will experience how this living God is personally involved and cares about the affairs of man. (Especially YOU...)

How does He do it? It's a mystery. But, I love watching it happen! You will too! Get ready for more testimonies than you know what to do with. Enjoy the journey and when you get finished, you'll want to begin again. I challenge you to do this very thing...maybe with your spouse, small group, or prayer group. It will change the atmosphere of your life, marriage, family, and/or church. It's a NOW time to *go for the gold in God.* To HIM be all the glory, honor, and praise!

❧ Endorsements ❧

Over 25 years ago I came under the tutelage of this mighty woman of God and learned that all those years since I was a child, that it was the Lord who had been speaking to me and showing me things. Sharon Mullins was instrumental in teaching me to recognize and release the prophetic gifting God had given me.

She has long been declaring the power of God's Word in prayer to see the Kingdom of Heaven released on earth. She seeks God's presence, hears from Him and prays His heart. This is her mission!

Over the years I have seen her train many others in this powerful engaging of the Believer's heart with God's to bring heaven to earth. Do you want to see change? Then begin declaring God's Word in faith! Begin by declaring these prayers that are straight from the Father's heart!

–Betty Kozloswki, Fellow intercessor and Deliverance minister

Shifting the Spiritual Atmosphere gave new meaning to prayer—from day one to day thirty, I was transformed and challenged. Sharon Mullins did an excellent job of bringing me into that place of prayer. These prayers release boldness for each new day; I came out of the prayer closet with a zeal, thirsts and boldness for God to reach the world each of us faces daily. I am looking forward to the journey I will experience reaching deep down within myself in this new book, Shifting the Spiritual Atmosphere 2. My desire is to continue to be transformed and challenged to do more in my life for God through prayer.

–Pastor Billy Gowan, Life Church, Monroe, North Carolina

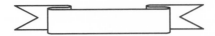

Sharon Mullins has been a great friend and mentor of mine for many years. Through her prayer life she has taught me how to pray effectively, preemptively and offensively. I want to ask, "What is the area of your life that you are really needing God to come through in? Where have you invested time, tears, and prayers—knowing that unless God moves you aren't going to make it?" God will come through!

In *Shifting the Spiritual Atmosphere 2*, these prophetic prayers will help each become more introspective and intimate with yourself and Jesus Christ. These prayers reach to the very depth of your being to allow Jesus to heal, prune, teach, comfort and open one's eyes to those things that have been hidden away. Investing time in prayer and God's word will never disappoint any. *Shifting the Spiritual Atmosphere 2* will transform the spiritual atmosphere within. I highly recommend this book.

–Pamela H. Tarlton, Monroe, North Carolina

☙ Testimonies ❧

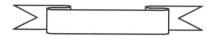

Please note that the following visitation took place after reading several of the prayers from my first book, Shifting the Spiritual Atmosphere. I felt it important to understand the significance of these prayers when declared aloud.

Sherrelle Giles' testimony, Rock Hill, South Carolina

Sharon Mullins gave me a copy of her new book on April 28, 2011. On October 11, 2011, I was watching Jonathan Welton, a seer on *It's Supernatural*, and prayed the prayer from Isaiah 6:8, "Whom shall I send, and who will go for us?" God asked me, "Will you go?" and my answer was **yes**.

Later that same evening I reached for Sharon's book, *Shifting the Spiritual Atmosphere, 30 prayers, 30 days, 30 minutes.* I was going through a difficult time and felt refreshed reading the chapters, one by one, out loud with full determination that what was being decreed, declared, and read would happen. Then I retired to bed.

The visitation began with a dream, although it may have been part of the visitation. (Dreams and visions are part of my life, but there have been fewer visitations.)

It started in bed. Something fell on my back, between my shoulder blades. I wiggled around to locate what had hit me. Grasping the object as it fell from my back, I saw that it was an *antiquated, used* flash bulb, used to take a picture. (*Indicating to me, picture this.*)

Immediately I heard voices talking together as they were entering my house through the back door. As they entered my kitchen, the voices grew quiet. Now I lay very still. It seemed there were a lot of men, from the sound of their voices. Then the sound of marching feet, doing double time—bump-bump, bump-bump—came down the long hallway. I saw a vision of them—rows of army military men—marching shoulder to shoulder, two together. As they passed my bedroom door, I was relieved that they continued toward the front door, turning to climb to the second floor. In the vision, I saw that these angels were intense and focused. They marched in unison. I lay very quietly hoping they would not discover the door to my bedroom. Who were they? In my visitation, it was so real, I believed it was happening in real-life. I was petrified like Daniel, and many of the people of the Bible. That's why so many angels of the Bible say, "Fear not!"

Then I heard it…a scratching at the threshold of my door. I froze as the door opened (Keep in mind, it was left open at night.) and they entered the room. Two very *tall* military men (angels) marched in and turned around and faced me standing at attention. My mind screamed, *"Why are they in my room? What are they going to do?"* My reaction was to draw the covers over my face.

Their army uniforms were olive green and brownish in color, made of a very heavy fabric. A helmet covered their heads. Their long-sleeved shirts and pants matched. The pant legs were tucked into very high boots that had heavy, thick soles. On their shoulders they carried big guns. Each of them had a belt and attached on the right side was a canteen full of water.

Immediately I awoke, stunned. No one was in my room. It was a **spiritual visitation** from the Lord, brought on by the prayers I had declared earlier in the evening. As I looked around my room I saw my door was open. What a relief!

I asked God what it all meant. *Why did the army of God come to my house, armed and ready for battle?*

He told me to go to the computer and locate the uniforms and find their army motto. I fell asleep and in the morning, I located similar uniforms and found the army motto to be, "This we'll defend!"

THIS WE WILL DEFEND! They came to protect me. God is so awesome.

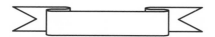

Linda Rushing's testimony, written with permission by Pamela H. Tarlton, Monroe, North Carolina

Linda was first diagnosed with bone cancer in her lower spine in January 2016. From January to April, she was only home one week. The rest of the time was in the hospital with three weeks in a rehabilitation facility. Enduring sixteen rounds of radiation, the local prayer group prayed constantly for her and began declaring prayers from the book, *Shifting the Spiritual Atmosphere,* over her. I gave her a copy of this book. She kept it, along with her Bible, with her at all times. Linda had a PET (Positron Emission Tomography) scan the first week of April 2016 and was declared cancer free. The doctors were amazed as her spine had also been splintered and this was also healed. The middle of April I had the chance to go see Pastor Pete and Sharon at a church they were speaking in Huntersville, NC. I told them about Linda and the prayers. I called Linda and let her tell her testimony herself over the phone to Pete and Sharon and the miracle God had done through the prayers.

In June of 2016 Linda's hip began to hurt her. The doctor told she had bone cancer once again and it was in her hip this time. The evil one was not giving up and neither was God nor Linda. She had another two months stay in the hospital, three weeks in rehabilitation, with a series of chemotherapy treatments. Once again, prayers, decrees and declarations went forth from *Shifting the Spiritual Atmosphere.* Linda was declared cancer free on November 4, 2016 and is not having the pain she had been nor the pain the doctors told her to expect after chemotherapy. GOD IS A MIRACLE WORKING AND COMPASSIONATE GOD! Only Jesus can do such things. HE shifts the spiritual atmosphere inside and out!

Shifting the Spiritual Atmosphere

30 Prayers ✸ 30 Days ✸ 30 Minutes

Part I

Individual Prayers with Journal

These prayers are designed to be spoken boldly, out loud and in a declarative manner. It is recommended that each prayer be personalized for the individual/couple/group that is praying. Be aware that God will inspire you to add whatever is on HIS heart for that specific time.

One
Completing the Work He Began

Dedicated to Steve and Charlotte Rutherford

"...being confident of this, that he who began a good work in you will carry it on to completion until the day of Christ Jesus" (Philippians 1:6 NIV).

1. *In this world there may be trouble, but be of good cheer; I have overcome the world* (John 16:33 paraphrased). In all this overcoming, there I stand in the midst of it...knowing that the good work You began in me will continue until it is completed. How my heart yearns for this. How I adore You with these thoughts: "Don't stop until You've completed the work. Don't allow the enemy to take me prematurely, before my time. Don't allow the continual wooing of the world and its ways to take the place of my longing for this completion to be accomplished."

2. I know that *You*, my Lord, *will never leave me nor forsake me* (Deut. 31:6). Yet, I see how Godly men and women have backslidden, and that makes me quake at the mere thought of it. I would rather tremble with the touch of Your hand, releasing me to my next assignment—the very thing I was created for.

3. How can I continue a moment longer without that reassurance? Yet, it is before me. The word of God has seared it in my brain; therefore, I continue to remain confident. *He who began a good work in me will not stop until it is completed* (Phil. 1:6 paraphrased). That thought brings me such comfort and overwhelms me to no end.

4. I know to him who has been given much, much is required (Luke 12:48 paraphrased). Once again, I bow my heart to the One and only— the King of Kings and Lord of Lords. I will not stop short of what You want of me. I will not allow my mind to become engaged otherwise.

5. I will continue to yield every thought, action, and deed to You and You alone. Take this offering and sanctify it, I pray. Take what You have given me; multiply it; bless it exponentially, and turn it into Your

likeness. I don't want to adore You from afar any longer. I want Your majesty to overwhelm me and You alone to be enthroned in my heart. I adore You.

6.   I invite You to come forth and overwhelm me once again. Just one touch...one breath...one moment, and I am never the same. Today I contend for that. I don't stop short. I contend also for that which You bought for me on the cross. I want to walk in the finished work. I want every drop of Your blood to be utilized to the fullest—nothing wasted.

7.   Teach me, Lord. I believe I can have it all. You give it freely to those that ask. You said that I could ask, seek, and find (Matt. 7:7 paraphrased). That is what I'm doing today. I'm asking. *(Do You hear me calling for more?)* I'm seeking. *(Can You feel my desperation?)* My goal is to find You and experience all of You that I can. I want it NOW—in the land of the living. I know it is possible. Teach me. Then, I will teach others. I will not hoard it to myself.

8.   Let me live a life that pleases You, my King, and these things that You have placed in my heart will become a reality—not just a prayer, a wish, a hope, or a dream. Circumcise my heart to all that You have for me.

9.   For the Word says—and I believe this for me, *He who began a good work will complete it* (Phil. 1:6 paraphrased). This is what I long for. This is what I ask. Help me rid myself of the dross of my life and receive You in all Your fullness to the absolute glory of God. Allow this request to resound in heaven as others join with me to become who God created each to be before the creation of the world, in Jesus' holy and precious name, Amen and amen.

What other prayers or thoughts has this prayer evoked from you to the Lord? Write them here.

_____

_____

_____

_____

_____

_____

_____

Journal personal notes, thoughts, prophetic words, and ideas you are hearing or sensing from the Lord. This may even include Scripture He is showing you.

_____

_____

_____

_____

_____

_____

_____

_____

_____

Two
Releasing the Secret Weapon
~ Righteous Anger

Dedicated to Craig, Lynn, and Jonathan Black and to all who stand up for righteousness when wickedness abounds

"My dear brothers, take note of this: Everyone should be quick to listen, slow to speak and slow to become angry, for man's anger does not bring about the righteous life that God desires" (James 1:19-20 NIV).

"So then, my beloved brethren, let every man be swift to hear, slow to speak, slow to wrath; for the wrath of man does not produce the righteousness of God" (James 1:19-20 NKJV).

"You have knowledge of this, dear brothers. But let every man be quick in hearing, slow in words, slow to get angry; for the righteousness of God does not come about by the wrath of man" (James 1:19-20 BBE).

"Understand this, my dear brothers and sisters: You must all be quick to listen, slow to speak, and slow to get angry. Human anger does not produce the righteousness God desires" (James 1:19-20 NLT).

1. Release it, for the time has come and is now that I must walk void of anger and allow peace which passes all understanding to be the evidence that You live in my heart and have transformed my life. My cry today is that I could rid myself of this fleshly anger and wear Your peace like a mantle. Let this mantel cover my mind and shield me from those things that would cause me or another to stumble.

2. Rid me of malice that would chase me and consume me…bringing bitterness, like bile, into every word I speak and think. I don't want these things; yet, they chase me when I least expect it. I am consumed by it rather than by You and Your presence. I cry out today that Your presence would be like a veil, covering my mind from the tormenter, and that his ways would be far from me. I want to be *quick to listen; I*

desire to be *slow to speak*; but, mostly I yearn to *be slow to anger* (James 1: 19 paraphrased).

3. Hear my confession; allow these words to penetrate the throne room of God. "I have not been *quick to listen, slow to speak, or slow to anger* (James 1:19 paraphrased). For this and more, I repent." I turn to You, the only One who is able to save to the utmost. With the help of the Holy Spirit, I know You will help me to walk in the righteousness of God.

4. I choose to allow YOU to infiltrate the places that no living person knows about—the deepest, darkest recesses of my soul that even I don't want to look upon. I release them to You, knowing that the cleansing work of the cross will penetrate. It is sufficient! Then and only then will I feel forgiven and free. I can now allow righteous anger to bubble forth.

5. Once You do this cleansing work, I will know it is the Holy Spirit who comes forth in me and not this soulish self that *wants what it wants when it wants it.* Only then can I trust myself when I feel the fury and experience the rage. Unrighteous anger and rage is not what I want. Even amid my sin and imperfection, this is the thing I long for: that You, my King and Lord, would rule every part of me: body, soul, and spirit.

6. Then, I will shout, cry, call out, and decree things that are pleasing to You—not what my flesh naturally gravitates to and is pleasing to me. Only then will I have the grace and confidence to do as You did, turning over the tables of the moneychangers and allowing righteous indignation and anger to have its proper place in me (Matt. 21:12 paraphrased).

7. Then, I will righteously rage for the lost and abused. Then, I will pray and defend the unborn—those facing abortion and those involved in all sorts of perversion. Then, I will cry out from the deepest depth of my heart and see You work miracles in this nation once again. Then, I will seek You, and Your face will be before my eyes. I will see that I am changed from glory to glory. How can this be? It's a *"BUT GOD"* moment.

8. As the purity of my prayers reach heaven, I know Your power is released and I am praying what is right <u>and</u> good <u>and</u> pleasing to You,

my Heavenly Father (Deut. 6:18 paraphrased). I want it to be You and not me. That's what I cry out today and release anger that is righteous and heavenly decreed, in Jesus' holy name. Amen.

What other prayers or thoughts has this prayer evoked from you to the Lord? Write them here.

_____

_____

_____

_____

_____

_____

_____

_____

Journal personal notes, thoughts, prophetic words, and ideas you are hearing or sensing from the Lord. This may even include Scripture He is showing you.

_____

_____

_____

_____

_____

_____

_____

_____

Three
You Are Our Refuge

Dedicated to Randy and Kim Colver

In you, O Lord, I have taken refuge; let me never be put to shame. Rescue me and deliver me in your righteousness; turn your ear to me and save me" (Psalms 71:1-2 NIV).

1. Abba, Father, I hear You say, *"Do not let your heart be troubled; neither let it be afraid."* (John 14:27 paraphrased). Even so, today I cry out to You. Hear me and vindicate me, Lord. Do not let the darkness of my soul overtake me. Push it back so all I can see is the light of Your presence. Surround me with Your light.

2. My ways are full of anguish and I cry out for help; yet no one hears or understands but You. Therefore, I take delight in You, my King; I pour out my heart before You like a drink offering. The suffering of my soul radiates from me and You alone know. Yet, I take heart because of the same fact: You know.

3. In You and You alone, I take refuge. I hide myself in You. I go deeper and deeper knowing that none can find me nor harm me as I lay on Your chest, wrapped in Your love. I stop, stay awhile, and meditate on You and Your covenant promises.

4. My cry echoes forth, "Let my thoughts be pure and of YOU and You alone." The longing for more of You continues forth in a prayer; "Come near to me, O God. Do not forsake me. Allow the richness of Your presence to overtake and overwhelm me."

5. I am thirsty for You. This thing called *life* is dry and I feel forsaken. But, I recall Your promise that *You will never leave me nor forsake me* (Deut. 31:6 paraphrased). Because of this, in the midst of the enemy's attack, I rest knowing *I will never be put to shame* (Ps. 25:3 paraphrased). I meditate on this, even though the frailties of my heart have a difficult time perceiving it. My mind apprehends it, knowing You bore that shame on the cross for me. Let this reality be my reality.

Let this truth penetrate until it reaches the uttermost parts of my mind, soul, and spirit. I yield to You. Help me, Lord.

6. I renounce and repent of entertaining spirits of darkness, oppression, depression, fear and dread. I don't want them and send them into the pit, commanding them never to return, in the mighty name of Jesus. I break all their assignments against me as I trust the One who is able to save to the uttermost (Heb. 7:25 paraphrased) and allow You to fill me fuller and fuller. I forsake pain, suffering, anguish, and thought patterns that lead me down this despicable path. I annihilate all this by the Name that's above every name and refuse it to ever return. I turn myself over to You—all the way.

7. "Allow the groans within me to burn forth into words that transcend this world into the throne room of God," I shout vehemently! Also, grant me words that are of significant tenderness, yet filled with passion and conviction that the heart of my Abba Daddy takes notice of and is moved by. May they produce such a heavenly stirring that His will is released in me and through me to eradicate all that the enemy has done in sowing seeds of discord and darkness.

8. May Your will strike such a symphony in my heart that I am now a living, walking, breathing representation of Heaven ...only doing, saying, and modeling what I see is taking place by my Heavenly Father. Let this delight transform everything about me. I will not stop until I see my transformation in the land of the living with my eyes. You are God, the Lover of my Soul...the Transformer of my nature...my Bright and Morning Star (Rev. 22:16 paraphrased). All that I need is found in You.

9. I trade my old ways for You. I go forward to reap the benefits sown through this prayer. I find glimmers of joy as the transforming power of Your presence changes me. My hope is in You and You alone. It overwhelms me and overtakes me. Finally, there is peace all around me. You carry me and I feel loved; You have turned Your ear to me and given solace to my soul. My salvation overtakes me and I can truly say, *"It is well with my soul."* Thank You, Lord, in the mighty name of Jesus. Amen.

What other prayers or thoughts has this prayer evoked from you to the Lord? Write them here.

_____

_____

_____

_____

_____

_____

_____

_____

Journal personal notes, thoughts, prophetic words, and ideas you are hearing or sensing from the Lord. This may even include Scripture He is showing you.

_____

_____

_____

_____

_____

_____

_____

_____

Four
Hearing Your Voice

Dedicated to Amanda Long and Lauren Trogdon

"Whether you turn to the right or to the left, your ears will hear a voice behind you, saying, "This is the way; walk in it. (Isaiah 30:21 NIV).

1. Father, today, I come to You in the mighty name of Jesus. My cries reach to heaven and I am set free more and more—every day, every hour, and every moment to be more of what You want me to be. I will not stop until I reach that thing for which I was created—destiny. I know that before the creation of the earth, You had a plan for my life. I believe and my mouth declares, *"It is good."*

2. I am about the Father's business. I believe and trust You for the fulfillment of this scripture. I know *whether I turn to the right or to the left,* it makes no difference because we serve an amazing and sovereign God. I hear a voice that leads and directs my path. I know which way to walk. I hear You. I obey You. Today, I thank You for directing my path. My plan is not north, south, east or west; it is the direction of God. You lead and direct my every step through dreams, visions, prophesies, and the Bible...all the time, every day. How awesome You are!

3. The paths of many take them to unknown places that lead to the valley of dry bones (Ez. 37:1 paraphrased). Not me! This is not where I want to be, so I listen to Your voice. I want to be directed every moment, every second, every hour, every day to the places that You have for me. Destiny is calling. Let me not waste one second traveling in the wrong direction and taking up false mantles or counterfeit ways. Pleasing my Savior is what drives me. I am driven by the One and only true God. Day in and day out, I walk in the unknown. Yet, I know it is firmly established and charted by the One who is able to save to the uttermost—my Savior and King!

4. Today, I declare to my ears, "Hearing, come forth in a way that keeps me attuned to the Lord. Senses, activate!" I yield all my senses to You. Would You touch my mouth to declare words that are sweet yet filled

with Heaven—released to the earth? Would You breathe Your breath through me? Would You allow my breath to be so mingled with Yours that a new oneness that I have never experienced before comes forth?

5. I declare this presence is tangible and noticeable, breaking chains of darkness within and without that I did not even know existed. I come into alignment with You and command all my senses to do the same. Daily, I sanctify them over and over again by Your Word and Your presence. My choice is You! No other will do.

6. Even my touch and smell notice new God fragrances and feel the tangible presence. How can they not when the God of the Universe orchestrates every move with a voice directing my path? Thank You for sanctified ears that hear Your voice directing me daily. I don't understand how this is all possible, yet, I surrender to You. As I go through the process, I understand more and more. Simultaneously, I care less and less for anything that's not all about You. I yield myself to Your will, Your plan, and Your ways.

7. This lovesick child releases *"all"* to You—believing, declaring, decreeing, and crying out, "Yes, there is a voice that I can hear that directs me every step of the way." Even past wrongs I've committed and past guilts that want to haunt me surrender to Your ways. I know everything I've ever done has brought me to this time and place. I now understand, with every fiber of my being, that You love me and direct me every inch of the way. Your plan unfolds before my eyes and I continually marvel at it. That which was impossible is now possible! For this I give You all glory, honor, and praise. I pray this in Your precious name…Jesus. Amen, amen, and amen.

What other prayers or thoughts has this prayer evoked from you to the Lord? Write them here.

_____

_____

_____

_____

_____

_____

_____

_____

Journal personal notes, thoughts, prophetic words, and ideas you are hearing or sensing from the Lord. This may even include Scripture He is showing you.

_____

_____

_____

_____

_____

_____

_____

_____

Five
Forgiveness

This is for all that have dedicated their lives to being un-offendable in the last days.

"Forgive us our debts, as we also have forgiven our debtors. And lead us not into temptation, but deliver us from the evil one. For if you forgive men when they sin against you, your heavenly Father will also forgive you. But if you do not forgive men their sins, your Father will not forgive your sins" (Matthew 6:12-15 NIV).

1. I yield my heart to You today. The things that have caused me pain try to light on me and remind me of my past failures. I declare, demanding freedom today, "I don't want this!" So, why are these thoughts here? Why do they remind me of things I don't want to remember? I forgive over and over; yet, my heart does not seem to align. So, once again, I forgive, knowing this will open the floodgates and allow my prayers to be unhindered and transcend this world to the throne room of God.

2. "I forgive!" is my cry. Because of these two words, my prayers come into agreement and alignment with the prayers that my Beloved Bridegroom and Great Intercessor is already making on my behalf. The hallowing of His name and the shouts of triumph echo forth as all of heaven hears and awaits the instruction of the Great Judge…my Abba Daddy. He hears the cries of His Son as He represents me in the courtroom of Heaven. The pleas and arguments come forth; the verdict goes out and angels are dispatched to do His bidding. Thank You for planting the initiative of forgiveness in me.

3. Even when others don't follow this path, I do. I do not allow myself the right to have rights. I have released them to You. I will burn with the passion to forgive whenever, whoever, wherever, and for whatever the need may demand. My eyes are upon You, my Lord and King. I have taken them off **my** hurt…**my** pain…**my** rights…**my** ways…**my** plans…**my** agenda…**my** options. I will not tire of seeking Your strength to do this. I declare this loudly as a constant reminder that I have given up the option to dwell on myself. My eyes are on You alone.

31

4. When I feel I can't go on, I stop. Then I seek Your presence and Your peace. This gives me the strength and courage I need. I pray that I will never allow thoughts to become so overwhelming that I give in to them and allow them to control me. I choose to have only one Master—YOU, **El Shaddai** (Lord God Almighty), **El Elyon** (The Most High God), **Adonai** (Lord, Master), **Yahweh** (Lord, Jehovah), **Jehovah Nissi** (The Lord My Banner), **Jehovah-Raah** (The Lord My Shepherd), **Jehovah Rapha** (The Lord That Heals), **Jehovah Shammah** (The Lord Is There), **Jehovah Tsidkenu** (The Lord Our Righteousness), **Jehovah Mekoddishkem** (The Lord Who Sanctifies You), **El Olam** (The Everlasting God), **Elohim** (God), **Qanna** (Jealous), **Jehovah Jireh** (The Lord Will Provide), **Jehovah Shalom** (The Lord Is Peace), and **Jehovah Sabaoth** (The Lord of Hosts).

5. You are the One who takes my breath away. With every beat of my heart, I trust You to help me align myself with You. I want to be all that You want me to be. The path of forgiveness leads and guides me. With heartfelt, real-life forgiveness active in me, I become the person God created me to be. I want to walk through life reaching my full potential. "Release"—that is my plea. I hear You clearly… "Forgive all and become unoffendable!"

6. "Yes," I cry; "Yes," to You. That is my goal. I can do this because You live inside of me. Allow Your spirit to teach me and guide me in the way I should go (Ps. 32: 8 paraphrased) …then and only then will I not depart from it. Even though the enemy has other plans and tries to get me off-track, I say, "No!" It is a violent and vehement NO—one that is decisive and causes me to do what is right. It forces a heavenly alignment to take place. My heart says, "Yes," but I still cry, "Help me Lord! Help! I choose to forgive and to be unoffendable, so that my prayers reach heaven" (Matt. 18:35 paraphrased). In the name of Jesus, Amen!

What other prayers or thoughts has this prayer evoked from you to the Lord? Write them here.

_____

_____

_____

_____

_____

_____

_____

Journal personal notes, thoughts, prophetic words, and ideas you are hearing or sensing from the Lord. This may even include Scripture He is showing you.

_____

_____

_____

_____

_____

_____

_____

_____

Six
Healing

Dedicated to Russell Long

"He sent his word, and healed them, and delivered them from their destructions" (Psalms 107:20 KJV).

"Surely he took up our infirmities and carried our sorrows, yet we considered him stricken by God, smitten by him, and afflicted. But he was pierced for our transgressions, he was crushed for our iniquities; the punishment that brought us peace was upon him, and by his wounds we are healed. (Isaiah 53:4-5 NIV).

"Surely he hath borne our griefs, and carried our sorrows: yet we did esteem him stricken, smitten of God, and afflicted. But he was wounded for our transgressions, he was bruised for our iniquities: the chastisement of our peace was upon him; and with his stripes we are healed" (Isaiah 53:4-5 KJV).

1. From the depths of my being to the highest of heights, I will praise You. I will sing out praise to You and for You, my God and King. How majestic are Your ways, O Lord. How incredible are Your thoughts toward me. I thank You in the midst of my situation that You are Jehovah Rapha, the Lord that heals.

2. Where can I go from You? If I go to the Heavens, You are there. If I flee to the depths, You are there" (Ps. 139:8 paraphrased). You are a living God. You heal me and see me through every difficult situation. You are the One that lays the path out before me and says, "*Whether you turn to the right or to the left, your ears will hear a voice behind you, saying, 'This is the way; walk in it'*" (Isa. 30:21 NIV).

3. I keep to Your path because I understand Your ways through Your word. You want to heal me; You want to deliver me from my own destructive ways and tendencies. Your path will lead me there. Your path took You to the cross to bear my iniquities and sorrow. The stripes You bore were given for me to gain access to all that You did

for me on the cross. My debt is paid in full. Thank you for these three small words, *"It is finished!"* (John 19:30 NIV).

4. I appropriate this complete work today—knowing that it is for me. I am healed. You made my innermost being, and all my days were numbered by You beforehand (Ps. 139: 16 paraphrased). You understand everything about me and love me just as I am. You gaze upon me and know that I am fearfully and wonderfully made (Ps. 139:14 paraphrased). I rejoice in this fact even when things in my body don't cooperate. I never give up on You.

5. In the midst of all this, I walk from facts (what the doctors and my body are reporting) into the truth—*by His stripes I am healed* (Is. 53:5 paraphrased). *He sent His word to heal me* (Ps. 107: 20 paraphrased). I look with spiritual eyes as best as I am able. I command my body to align with all that is true, right, and good. I don't lie; yet, I trust the One who died on the cross for me. It is the finished work in which I place my hope, belief, and trust.

6. Your word says, and I believe it, *"Surely he hath borne our griefs, and carried our sorrows: yet we did esteem him stricken, smitten of God, and afflicted. But he was wounded for our transgressions, he was bruised for our iniquities: the chastisement of our peace was upon him; and with his stripes we are healed"* (Isa. 53:4-5 KJV).

7. What could be better than Your word applied to my situation? My mind perceives it, but how do I receive it in actuality? It is such a mystery. It is the mystery of the cross and Your Kingdom…an understanding that You did a complete work. I cry out and pray to know how to receive all that You did for me. So, daily I plead with my Savior, "Teach me how to pray; teach me how to receive!" You are the God who heals me. You are God, and in You is <u>no lack</u>.

8. This imperfect vessel cries out to walk in this, fulfilling that which You fulfilled at the cross. "Please help me," is my cry! "I am unable to ascertain this unless You help me." Then peace comes, and I know You have heard my supplication. *"Thy will be done on earth as it is in Heaven"* (Matt. 6:10 KJV). Even amid this trial, I choose not to stress; instead I receive Your peace, which *passes all understanding (Phil. 4:7 paraphrased).* I will seek more of You daily with every breath and all my being! In the name of Jesus, Amen.

What other prayers or thoughts has this prayer evoked from you to the Lord? Write them here.

_____

_____

_____

_____

_____

_____

_____

Journal personal notes, thoughts, prophetic words, and ideas you are hearing or sensing from the Lord. This may even include Scripture He is showing you.

_____

_____

_____

_____

_____

_____

_____

_____

_____

Seven
Let's Not Grow Weary

Dedicated to Karen Fraley Coey and Becky Sparks Hitchens

"And let us not be weary in well doing: for in due season we shall reap, if we faint not" (Gal. 6:9 KJV).

"Anyone, then, who knows the good he ought to do and doesn't do it, sins" (James 4:17 NIV).

1. Speak, declare, shout, and sing to all who have ears to hear, **"I serve a holy God."** The Lord tells me to be holy for He is holy! (1Pt. 1:16 paraphrased). Therefore, I take this approach to all things to the best of my ability. I stand ready to decree Your word and wait for it to perform all that You intend for the Word to perform. I do not...I cannot...I will not...grow "weary in well doing" (Gal. 6:9 KJV).

2. My eyes are upon You, Most High God and King. Therefore, I take the Word of God seriously. I don't want to sin. I confess my sins when I do. I can't escape this one thing...if I know what I'm supposed to be doing (the Bible teaches me this) and yet I do otherwise, then I have sinned (James 4:17 paraphrased). Lord, this is so easy to understand, but so difficult to do.

3. Everywhere I look, I see the opposite taking place. Therefore, my cry to You is for HELP! Your word tells me to be quick to listen (James 1:19 paraphrased). How do I do this? Habits are set up in my life and take me to a place of valuing my thoughts and ways rather than Your truth. I repent, seek Your face, and turn from my ways to Yours.

4. Help me be slow to speak so that my words don't become lofty and I suffer the same fate as Job's friends. Allow the words that come forth to be like the *pen of a ready writer.* (Ps. 45:1 paraphrased) ...*apples of sliver in settings of gold* (Pr. 25:11 NIV) ...not mere words that accomplish nothing but oppress the listener and fall to the ground. They are of no value. Allow my words to be what's on God's heart and in tune with the symphony of heaven: on key, pleasing and full of melodious sounds that come together like a symphony to the hearers.

5. The ways of the world can cause my blood to boil with anger and frustration. Yet, Your word warns me: *be slow to become angry* (Js. 1:19 paraphrased). I say, "Yes," and try to heed that; but, I hear of the atrocities against the unborn and the defamation against my Lord and Savior. I can barely take it. So, I ask You to teach me the difference between righteous anger and anger that erupts from my soul. My soul produces that which pleases the flesh and can be demonic in its origin—producing sinful responses; yet, righteous anger is in sync with heaven and reverberates Biblical wisdom from God, my Creator. My goal is to bring delight to You...help me be one who goes above and beyond to please You, King Jesus.

6. Holy Spirit, I need Your guidance and grace to traverse this. I don't want to be fleshly driven, giving into the anger that loves to burn and spew forth words that do not bring pleasure to heaven and its host. Holy Spirit, help me and allow my spirit to connect to You instead of my fleshly ways and nature.

7. Everywhere I look people defame the name of God, using it with such ignorance, distaste and ingratitude. I cry out, "Help me do the opposite, being one who brings glory to Your name, rightly dividing the word of God (2 Tim. 2:15 paraphrased) and expressing truth to a lost and dying people." May my words be heavenly inspired—supernatural in character, producing swift results...Let the consequence of my words be eternal in disposition—making a difference on this earth and forever. It's all about YOU! May I truly live Your Word and do what is right. May I be a doer of Your Word so that I walk, talk, and act uprightly...in a way that pleases You. Help me have words that are sweet going out to the hearer. Help, Abba Daddy. This is my cry; this is my plea, and I ask it in the mighty, magnificent name of Jesus. Amen.

What other prayers or thoughts has this prayer evoked from you to the Lord? Write them here.

_____

_____

_____

_____

_____

_____

_____

_____

Journal personal notes, thoughts, prophetic words, and ideas you are hearing or sensing from the Lord. This may even include Scripture He is showing you.

_____

_____

_____

_____

_____

_____

_____

_____

Eight
You can Run; but You Can't Hide...

Dedicated to Emily Fauk, Betty Kozlowski, Jacqueline Teagle, Nancy Hughes and Paul Schneider

"But if I drive out demons by the Spirit of God, then the kingdom of God has come upon you" (Matt. 12:28 NIV).

"But if I drive out demons by the finger of God, then the kingdom of God has come to you" (Luke 11:20 NIV).

1. I stand amazed in Your presence, Lord! I stand amazed that You would ever consider using me to advance Your Kingdom. Yet, in this one name...JESUS (of Nazareth) ...demons tremble and flee; sickness is healed; people are saved! The Kingdom of God advances and is released. So, I choose today to scream it out (JESUS), shout it from the rooftops (JESUS), declare it at the top of my lungs (JESUS). Your name is precious and powerful...JESUS!

2. I can feel it. The earth responds. There is trembling, shaking, shifting, and stirring. There is gasping, breathing, begging, and birthing. This happens every time Your name is whispered, spelled, spoken, or shouted. All of it produces Your good will and pleasure (Phil. 2:13 paraphrased). Yeah! I get to be a part of it. You choose me whether I'm having a good day or bad—whether I'm happy or sad. I see it and shout it out! "It's all about You every day, all the time, and in every way!" What an awesome God I serve!

3. This is what I hear and come into agreement with. *"On your mark, get set, go!"* That's how I start each day. Anticipation for what lies ahead summons me, and I say "Yes!" I know that wherever I go, my footsteps cause realms to stir and shift. I take ground for God because You live in me. Every place I go is a chance to advance the Kingdom. I pray, "Give me eyes to see and ears to hear. Help me make the most of every opportunity—doing and praying what is on the Father's heart."

4. I step out, laying hands on the sick, praying for the lost, and casting out demons. Freely I have received, so freely I give (Matt. 10:8 paraphrased). Lord, I stand ready—like a good soldier. I want to hear You as never before and do specifically what You're saying. Obedience is the key. Help me not strike out, but to hit the target. Help me to know when to speak and when to remain silent.

5. Teach me how to pray what's on Your heart, not mine. Help me to understand the supernatural and how to operate within the heavenly guidelines and parameters. I long to drive out demons and *know that I know* that the Kingdom of God has advanced. I want to pray the most effective way...getting to the answer by going the quickest route.

6. Evil entities lurk, waiting and hiding. They know I'm coming for them. They may run and hide, but, I operate in the gifts of the spirit—the weapons of my warfare. My tool belt is full and ready for use at a moment's notice. It could be in church, on the phone, in a prayer meeting, at a restaurant or possibly while shopping. I thank You, Lord, that You have trained my hands and fingers for battle (Ps. 144:1 paraphrased) and I am an able warrior. You have taught me how to make surgical strikes, so I cry out and You answer...The results: ***another demon bites the dust!***

7. Daily You hear my pleas and answer my prayers. So I cry out, "Use me to advance Your Kingdom, to set the captives free." I want to feel the presence of my King and God! How lovely You are! Surely You have chosen me. I see it happening continually...demons are driven out by the spirit of God that lives within me. Selah! I pause to consider...why would the God of the Universe ever consider using me, a mere mortal? It is unbelievable...incredible...unfathomable. I stand in awe and give thanks. It's all I've ever wanted, and Your answer is "YES!" What more can I say, except thank You for allowing me to participate with You in these supernatural endeavors, in the mighty name of Jesus! Amen.

What other prayers or thoughts has this prayer evoked from you to the Lord? Write them here.

_____

_____

_____

_____

_____

_____

_____

_____

Journal personal notes, thoughts, prophetic words, and ideas you are hearing or sensing from the Lord. This may even include Scripture He is showing you.

_____

_____

_____

_____

_____

_____

_____

_____

Nine
Opening Doors that no Man Can Shut

Dedicated to Pete II and Erika Mullins, and David and Catherine Robbins

"These things says he who is holy, he who is true, he who has the key of David, opening the door so that it may be shut by no one, and shutting it so that it may be open to no one" (Rev. 3:7 BBE).

1. Father, I come today, holding a prayer key—the key of David. I don't want anything but Your will to be done in my life and those I love. Yet, sometimes *Your will* evades me. I don't know what to pray. I don't know what to say or ask for. I don't have the solution.

2. Yielding all to You, I simply pray, "Would You open Your door of destiny for _____ (name your church), my family, and me? (Name any situation or specific door that needs to be opened at this time.) My plea to heaven resounds. Would You close every door that is not Your plan? Would it be such that no man could open it once You've closed it; and no man can close it once You've opened it?" (Rev. 3:7 paraphrased). In other words, let it be only Your will coming forth. I am no longer satisfied with your permissive will. I must walk in the perfect will of God.

3. My flesh wants to interfere in this process. It is weak. Yet, I know that Your strength in my life is what I need. Therefore, I set my face like flint, trusting You in the midst of my weakness and every circumstance. I choose to believe You for the outcome. Help me to seek You in all things, realizing, *"Your grace **IS** sufficient!"* (2 Cor. 12:9 paraphrased).

4. I shout for all to hear, "I serve God!"—the One who is **all**-seeing, **all**-knowing, **all**-powerful, and **ever**-present. He alone gives me keys that bring heaven to earth…*His will, not mine*…the sufficiency of all that is needed at the exact right time for every circumstance.

5. I do my best to back off and remove my hands from the situation. *(HELP ME DO THIS, LORD!)* I Cast this upon the Lord, and my

prayers release the King of Kings and Lord of Lords. You are arranging things on my behalf, doing only what You see the Father doing; saying only what is right and glorious—what the Father is saying (John 5:19 paraphrased).

6. My plea reaches heaven, opening and closing doors—heaven comes to earth. My faith arises as I look into the eyes of my Beloved. Your perfect will, not mine… Your ways, not some fleshly desire. How magnificent this is! I am completely abandoned to the One who bought my salvation. I realize this is for my good, but mostly for Your glory.

7. Ultimately, I yield myself and every situation to You…this makes all the difference. Once again, I see that Your ways are higher than mine. You respond to the sound of my voice, causing my situations to bow and align with heaven as I pray, releasing the key of David. I watch in delight as God hooks eternity into the here and now. Come, Holy Spirit! Help me to know when to pray this. Guide me into all truth. Thank You for this tool…this key…this prayer, in Jesus' name, Amen.

What other prayers or thoughts has this prayer evoked from you to the Lord? Write them here.

_____

_____

_____

_____

_____

_____

_____

_____

Journal personal notes, thoughts, prophetic words, and ideas you are hearing or sensing from the Lord. This may even include Scripture He is showing you.

Ten
Rejoice in the Lord Always

Dedicated to Kathy Peters and my sacred sisters—Wanda Mardis, Diane Calsbeek, Darlene Lovett, and Stacey Smith

"Rejoice in the Lord always. I will say it again: Rejoice!" (Phil. 4:4 NIV).

1. Today is a day of rejoicing! That is my choice. I choose to rejoice in You, my Lord and King…in all You are…in all You've done…I will not stop rejoicing until it reaches heaven and I see a smile on Your face. All You've done has made me glad. I refrain from dwelling on other things—incomplete and undone work lying before me. My thoughts are on You and You alone.

2. I have seen You do great and mighty things. This is cause for celebration. I have seen You come forth as the One Who Battles and Wins Victories on my behalf. I have seen You as the One Who Promises and Delivers…the One Who is Silent, saying, "Not now, My child." Yet, this is for my good, but ultimately for Your glory."

3. Lord, I adore You with all that I am today. I enthrone You in my heart once again. I give You permission to release the fresh oil for today. I am so full of thanksgiving that my heart explodes and pours forth pure love for You, the Lover of my soul. Nobody can take this away from me; my spiritual roots go down deep and wide. False winds of doctrine cannot dissuade me. No…the fire of God burns bright within me. You see this and remain glad.

4. My delight is in You. This transforms every part of me, bringing a divine connection. All that are around me wonder what it is. It's not *what but WHO*…the Bridegroom. That's why I continue to make myself ready (Rev. 19:7 paraphrased), rejoicing day and night in YOU! My lamp is full of oil; the Holy Spirit is alive and active in me. I sense Your presence. My spirit leaps with joy.

5. Thanks for all that You do in and through me. I know that the Kingdom of God advances. It is here—within and around me. When I

step out, ground is taken for the Kingdom. The enemy retreats as I rejoice. How cool is that? Thank You, Jesus, for marvelous times of rejoicing in You and through You, bringing me one step closer to destiny fulfilled and the promise of my salvation being realized. What a time of rejoicing, in the mighty name of Jesus, amen and amen!

W hat other prayers or thoughts has this prayer evoked from you to the Lord? Write them here.

_____

_____

_____

_____

_____

_____

_____

_____

J ournal personal notes, thoughts, prophetic words, and ideas you are hearing or sensing from the Lord. This may even include Scripture He is showing you.

_____

_____

_____

_____

_____

_____

_____

_____

Eleven
Destiny is the Goal

Dedicated to Sherrelle Giles, Jonathan and Mary Beth Mullins

"Yet I still belong to you; you hold my right hand. You guide me with your counsel, leading me to a glorious destiny. Whom have I in heaven but you? I desire you more than anything on earth" (Ps. 73:23-25 NLT).

1.   Lord, how I praise and adore You. Allow my voice to be clear and sustained, like that of a youth—even into my latter years. Allow praise, glory, adoration, worship, teaching, and preaching to come forth and ring out for all to hear. Don't allow the trailing of my voice and vocal weariness ever to be something that stops what You have placed in me to do.

2.   I say, "Voice, come forth in strength, power, and might" that all may hear and know that I serve the One True God, and that He has given me something to preach, pray, and sing about! I worship You, Almighty God; there is NONE like You!

3.   My heart rejoices in this thought! So, I declare it for all to hear and know. I will not be silenced when it comes to the King of Kings and Lord of Lords! You alone are worthy…You alone are worthy…You alone are worthy! I command even my vocal cords to align with the purposes and plans of the Kingdom of God. Let me never grow weary in well doing.

4.   Coughing must cease. Laryngitis must go. Allergies and asthma must desist. Sore throat, tiredness, vocal pain, cancer and/or nodules of any type must bow to the name of Jesus and the finished work of the cross. I command *Destiny Stealer* to get off my vocal cords, out of my throat, and away from me. I will not give into demonic forces, nor will I sit idly by while *it* comes to rob, destroy, kill, or steal from me or any of God's children who are working out their salvation and God-ordained destiny. This is not optional.

5.   I sit up, take notice, and fight for that which Jesus fought for me and obtained. It happened in an instant when He said, "It is finished" (John

19:30 NIV). I come into agreement with this and receive what this means in Heaven while I'm still on the earth. My plea is simple... "Let not one jot or tittle go unfinished that God had planned for me before the creation of the world (Eph. 1:4 paraphrased). Let every breath within me breathe for one purpose and one purpose alone: may Your will be done on earth through me as it is in Heaven (Matt. 6:10 paraphrased)—nothing more...nothing less...Your will and Your will alone."

6. My cry today is that "Destiny" would be achieved in my life and that every hindrance would be thwarted right now...now and forever. Strength is one of the virtues I put on as a mantle. It allows me to be sustained in youth, middle age, or as a senior citizen. Let the beauty of Your holiness continue to flow through me as I walk with integrity and uprightness—clothed in You. This is my mantle of distinction.

7. I live fearlessly for You. This comes forth loud and clear. Those who know me marvel at what You're doing and saying through me, a vessel set apart to You. I hear and believe, *"The sky's the limit."* I respond with vigor, filled with anticipation, yet laced with humility as I take Your hand and call out, "Come on Jesus! Let's do this thing called Destiny together." You echo back my name with a holy, "Yes!"

8. As I kneel before You in adoration, I can hardly believe that You want to use me, and the only goal You have is that I fulfill what You created me to do. It's like a hand-in-glove...destiny. That's my goal and my prayer, in the mighty name of Jesus. Destiny, arise and come forth! Amen.

What other prayers or thoughts has this prayer evoked from you to the Lord? Write them here.

_____

_____

_____

_____

_____

_____

_____

Journal personal notes, thoughts, prophetic words, and ideas you are hearing or sensing from the Lord. This may even include Scripture He is showing you.

_____

_____

_____

_____

_____

_____

_____

_____

Twelve
Sowing and Reaping

Dedicated to Donna Smith

"Do not be deceived: God cannot be mocked. A man reaps what he sows. The one who sows to please his sinful nature, from that nature will reap destruction; the one who sows to please the Spirit, from the Spirit will reap eternal life. Let us not become weary in doing good, for at the proper time we will reap a harvest if we do not give up. Therefore, as we have opportunity, let us do good to all people, especially to those who belong to the family of believers" (Gal. 6:7-10 NIV).

1. Heavenly Father, Your ways are so much higher than mine; Your thoughts above what I can think or imagine (Is. 55:8 paraphrased). But, this one thing I do, I put behind me all that is not YOU and press forward to the calling that You have for me and me alone. I press to obtain the fullness of You (Phil. 3:13-14 paraphrased). Therefore, I rid myself of the former things…the old ways, to take up what is on Your heart for today.

2. I can only imagine what You have in store for me when I'm about what pleases the Father. My imagination runs wild thinking of ways to please my Abba Daddy. Knowing that Your word commands, "Do not be deceived," (Gal. 6:7 NIV) that is a key for all who have ears to hear. I look around and see so many who fail to obey and then reap a whirlwind of destruction. Don't let that be me, Lord. I don't want anything I do to mock or displease You. I do not delight in the resulting devastation that is produced.

3. I repent of sowing to *me, myself, and I*—that ugly, sinful nature that demands its way and produces a self-fulfilling prophecy of heartache and pain that results in ruin to my loved ones and me. My heart is set on doing right; but, when I least expect it, deception seizes me. It engulfs, entraps, and ensnares me. It produces the vilest results that I do not want. My cry to this lack of self-discipline and self-control is, "NO!" I am no longer availing myself to the spirits behind this lukewarm attitude and wickedness.

4. Instead, I yield my members to righteousness leading to holiness—sowing to please the Holy Spirit of Almighty God, my Comforter and Teacher. You are the only One whom I desire to please. You are the One who whispers, "Come up higher," and I respond with a wholehearted, "Yes!" I combine this with action. Words without deeds are empty and fall to the ground. That is not who I am!

5. I love on You, Jesus, with bold and speedy obedience, doing good to all people, knowing that I am laying up for myself Heavenly treasure that will not rust or fade. Rather, I produce what You intend; I do not become weary in well-doing or get easily sidetracked. My heart breaks for those who *talk the talk*, but do not *walk the walk—unfaithful to the core*—yet wanting to do right.

6. Hearts are hardened, fraught with the potholes of life brought about by deception—not understanding that there is a Biblical law in place called *sowing and reaping*. How can a loving God allow this? Your word says plainly, *"God cannot be mocked"* (Gal. 6:7 NIV). (That means You **will not** be…it is a supernatural impossibility!) My plea is that I have the grace to continually walk in the Holy Spirit *dunamis* power living in me to do what is right and pleasing to You. "Help me not be deceived, O Lord!" This cry goes out for my family, church, and friends also.

7. Help me not give up due to past failures. *Your mercies are new every morning* (Lam. 3:23 paraphrased). I receive it for today. I receive it for every moment of temptation. I open my eyes and walk in wisdom, sowing to the Spirit and reaping the benefits. Allow me to recognize and activate Your will for me at all times. I know it will lead to a rich harvest of well doing. This spills over to the family of believers, and is one of the ways I walk in God's plan for my life. Help me to be known as one who is about the Father's business, *"doing good,"* especially to the body of Christ.

8. Thank You, Lord, for spelling it out clearly so that I can understand Your ways. I thank You *for making a way when there seems to be no way* and helping me *walk the walk* You have for me. I praise You for this in the mighty and fabulous name of Jesus! Amen.

What other prayers or thoughts has this prayer evoked from you to the Lord? Write them here.

_____

_____

_____

_____

_____

_____

_____

Journal personal notes, thoughts, prophetic words, and ideas you are hearing or sensing from the Lord. This may even include Scripture He is showing you.

_____

_____

_____

_____

_____

_____

_____

_____

Thirteen
Delight Yourself in the Lord

Dedicated to Ashley Schultz and Cheryl Hanson

Trust in the LORD and do good; dwell in the land and enjoy safe pasture. Delight yourself in the LORD and he will give you the desires of your heart. Commit your way to the LORD; trust in him and he will do this: He will make your righteousness shine like the dawn, the justice of your cause like the noonday sun. Be still before the LORD and wait patiently for him (Ps. 37:3-7 NIV).

1. Abba, Daddy…I stop and pause at this one thought…this one insight, *"Delight yourself in the Lord"* (Ps. 37:4 NIV). Do I even have the slightest idea of how to do this? My cry today is, "Teach me to delight myself in You." Show me how to bring You *great enjoyment and pleasure*—the dictionary definition of *delight*.

2. My heart is fully devoted to this one thing today: bringing pleasure to You, my King. I begin my day basking in the sunlight of that thought. It warms my insides and my spirit-man comes alive. Even my heartbeat speeds up as I come into agreement with this scripture. I prayerfully question the One who can save to the uttermost, "What is required of me, and how do I do it?" If I think too long, I may become overwhelmed. What do I possess that I can present a king, especially the King of Kings?

3. Your word cajoles me: *"delight yourself in the Lord."* Then, I will *receive the desires of my heart.* (Ps. 37:4 paraphrased). Is that the goal? At first-glance it appears so. These heart-desires have been put there by You anyway. Yet, that is *so not* **it**, even though it transpires. First and foremost, it is Your breath in me, Your loving kindness flowing through me, and Your mercy toward me, which I receive as I delight in You. It's Your presence. It's the encounter of the living-ness of the living God. It is a touch from Heaven reaching into my being and the finger of God bringing exactly what is needful—YOU. This is what I want; this is my prayer; this is the essence of delighting in You. Other things come forth, but they are only secondary to an encounter with the King of Glory.

4. Of course, I long to obtain the desires of my heart that You have placed within me. But there is *more,* and I want the ***more***. This comes because I choose freely to accept the discipline of delighting in the *Alpha and Omega, the First and the Last, the Beginning and the End* (Rev. 22:13 NIV), *who is, and was and who is to come…* (Rev. 1:8 NIV). I do this with help from the Holy Spirit, even when I don't feel like it. I decree what is <u>not so</u>, so that in God's timing <u>it will be so</u>! That's what I'm releasing in faith today.

5. As I linger in prayer, You answer. It is, "Yes." I have asked to be taught and You have done it as I've pleaded, sought, and waited. My mind cannot comprehend this; yet, my spirit leaps with joy, drinking in Your presence, thirsting for more of You. My spirit connects with Your spirit and I receive a touch from the Lord. I want more. I want to be clothed with this tangible presence all the time. "Help me," I cry out.

6. And so You do. But, it begins with me. I must delight in You. Daily, I cry out for accelerated ability to delight in You in greater measure. Release this in exponential ways! The desires of my heart change as I obey this scripture. As I go forward, I ask less and less for the carnal things of this world. I appreciate the blessings that pour forth from a life well-lived *for* You and *by* You and *through* You. But more than that, I long and pant for the pure pleasure of Your presence which You bring as I delight in You.

7. I cry out for the tangible and the supernatural presence of Almighty God. Hear me as I call. Your answer is so simple…"Take delight in me," You say, "And surely I will give you the desires of your heart (Ps. 37:4 paraphrased). Don't be surprised if these desires change along life's journey." I am fascinated by this and continue my plea for help. I can't thank You enough, but I try to as I experience this newfound joy, freedom, and tangible presence that comes. I am forever thankful to my Abba Daddy, in the mighty name of Jesus. Amen.

What other prayers or thoughts has this prayer evoked from you to the Lord? Write them here.

_____

_____   _____

_____

_____

_____

_____

_____

Journal personal notes, thoughts, prophetic words, and ideas you are hearing or sensing from the Lord. This may even include Scripture He is showing you.

_____

_____

_____

_____

_____

_____

_____

_____

Fourteen
His Grace is Sufficient

Dedicated to Cathy Goddard, Julie Hunt, and Marilyn and Ray Boyle, my mother and late step-father

"To keep me from becoming conceited because of these surpassingly great revelations, there was given me a thorn in my flesh, a messenger of Satan, to torment me. Three times I pleaded with the Lord to take it away from me. But he said to me, "My grace is sufficient for you, for my power is made perfect in weakness" (2 Cor. 12:7-9 NIV).

1. I cry out to You, my Abba Father, Daddy, in the one and only mighty magnificent name, Jesus…knowing, declaring, and pleading Your word over my situation. The day appears bleak and uninviting. The enemies of my soul stand ready to pounce if I display the slightest weakness. They do not realize that my weakness is only an opportunity for the manifest strength of God to be released (1Cor. 12:9 paraphrased).

2. Releasing demonic plans at just the right moment and creating a whirlwind of absolute destruction, their objective is to distract me and bring unequivocal defeat. The target: annihilation of all that I was created for and all I've lived toward achieving—God's DESTINY for me. The demonic end-game: to not finish the race God has set before me.

3. It is the perfect storm, sent to separate me from the Lord—my beloved Bridegroom, neutralizing all that His blood bought. Yet, I stand unafraid, knowing that the *testing of my faith produces perseverance* (James 1:3 paraphrased). I will finish this race! Praying, I quote the word and stand on it, *"Your grace **IS** sufficient for me!"* (2 Cor. 12: 9 paraphrased). I shout it from the housetops for all to hear, "I will not back down; I will not give in; I will not relinquish ground!" I bellow it to all the attackers, seen and unseen, **"Do you hear me?"**

4. My Abba Daddy does. My Bridegroom does. The Holy Spirit does. All three coordinate their efforts. Jesus, at the right hand of the Father, is making intercession for me. He says and does only what God the

Father is saying and doing. The Holy Spirit honors the rest of the Godhead by illuminating God's plans through me, a mere mortal. The living-ness of God on the earth flows to me, in me and through me. I am not defeated! I am more than a conqueror. I know it. I believe it. I shout it. I decree it. I don't stand in God's way. My body, soul, and spirit come into agreement with the blueprints of Heaven.

5. I am not defeated! I am alive with Your presence. The forces of darkness may try to destroy me, but my prayers are like a wall that surrounds me. God protects me with all the might of heaven. Is it in the form of light? Is it the very essence of His presence…His anointing...His glory? Is it the angelic host sent to minister to those who will inherit salvation? Is it warring angels? Is it all of this or a combination? I don't know.

6. When I ask, You come. When I seek, You are found (Matt. 7: 7-8 paraphrased). God stands and knocks. I open. You come in; we sup together (Rev. 3:20 paraphrased). How can that be? My cry is, "Help." You say, "Yes!" Your word is performed. It is You, not me. Your presence comes. It's a mystery my mind cannot comprehend. It is the sufficiency of Your grace manifest in manifold ways, full of wisdom from on high, released to the here and now… Your word performed in the land of the living.

7. Yes, I'm a walking-talking-breathing example. *Your grace is sufficient for me . . . Your grace is sufficient for me . . . Your grace is sufficient for me . . .* (2 Cor. 12:9 paraphrased). That is the truth, and I thank You for all You've done in Jesus' mighty name. Amen.

What other prayers or thoughts has this prayer evoked from you to the Lord? Write them here.

_____

_____

_____

_____

_____

_____

_____

_____

Journal personal notes, thoughts, prophetic words, and ideas you are hearing or sensing from the Lord. This may even include Scripture He is showing you.

_____

_____

_____

_____

_____

_____

_____

_____

_____

Fifteen
God is for Us

Dedicated to Patrick and Sipra Singh

"What shall we then say to these things? If God be for us, who can be against us? He that spared not his own Son, but delivered him up for us all, how shall he not with him also freely give us all things?" (Rom. 8:31-32 KJV).

1. I read it, declare it and come into agreement with Romans 8:31-32 **now**. If God be for me *(He is!)*, who can be against me? The enemy tries in many ways, setting traps to ensnare me; the world beckons me to come hither; yet in reality, I am the only one who can open the door to sin and allow it in. Thank You, Lord, that nothing can be against me…but me.

2. *My spirit is willing, but my flesh is weak* (Mark 14:38 paraphrased). Therefore, I cry out for what I see within me and those around me. I know You love Your Church and bride. So today, I release over myself, my family, (name your church) _____, and all Christian believers everywhere, the ability to comprehend and grasp that God is truly in love with His Church. He wants all to be included.

3. Let it be an individual and corporate revelation. Start with me! Let it go forth from the pages of scripture to my mind, written on my heart. Allow this understanding to penetrate deeply. May it produce a life of action dedicated to King Jesus. My spirit-man connects with heaven and the response is, "Yes!"

4. I want all that You have for me. I want to stand in the midst of every situation—even in the fray of the battle—knowing that the God of the universe is for me, fighting my battles, tending to my wounds, whispering words of love, and anointing me with the oil of gladness. It is not beyond receiving; but it is too much for my mind to comprehend. Wrapped in the holiness of His arms, I shout again, "Yes, I want You and all that You have for me!"

5.   I want to delight in the pleasure of knowing You and sensing the slightest move You make. You are God; there is none that compares with You! Help me to grasp *how wide and long and high and deep is the love of Christ* (Eph. 3:18 NIV) for me! My prayer is that somehow I will be able to worship and adore You every moment with all that I am.

6.   Please receive this offering. With all my might I struggle to give it as freely as You gave Your Son, and as freely as You laid down Your life for me. I want my actions to match my words. Even so, You understand the frailty of my soul. When I am weak, You are strong (2 Cor. 12:9 paraphrased). When I sabotage my life with sin, You stand ready to forgive. As soon as I repent, You don't remember my sin any longer. With just one glance I am forgiven…restored totally to wholeness, as if I'd never sinned. How can this be?

7.   Over and over I long for more of You. I want to know You. I want to feel Your breath upon me and Your fire within me. This is my prayer. Let my life exist for You; let all that know me see YOU. Allow my life to be a living epistle that draws others to You and brings them into this same love relationship.

8.   How I love You and long to love You more and more. I meditate on You. My mind races to receive that You are for me all the time (Rom. 8:31 paraphrased) in every circumstance; no demon power from hell can stop that fact! I don't feel worthy to be the recipient of love this amazing; yet it is part of the everlasting covenant that You made with Your blood. Thank You does not seem to be enough. So, I say a simple three-letter word over and over, louder and louder, to communicate to the King of Glory a life-attitude for which there are not adequate human words to express: "Yes…Yes…YES!" Please accept this yes, in the name of Jesus I pray, Amen!

What other prayers or thoughts has this prayer evoked from you to the Lord? Write them here.

_____

_____

_____

_____

_____

_____

_____

Journal personal notes, thoughts, prophetic words, and ideas you are hearing or sensing from the Lord. This may even include Scripture He is showing you.

_____

_____

_____

_____

_____

_____

_____

_____

Sixteen
The Prayer of the Bride to the Bridegroom

Dedicated to Amanda and Russell Long, Gary and Shelly Davis, Paul Schneider, Julie Chambliss, and all who long for revival and kingdom transformation.

"Hallelujah! For our Lord God Almighty reigns. Let us rejoice and be glad and give him glory! For the wedding of the Lamb has come, and his bride has made herself ready. Fine linen, bright and clean, was given her to wear." (Fine linen stands for the righteous acts of the saints.) (Rev. 19:6-8).

1. Today I pray a love song to the One I adore...I come as the bride, arrayed in white...one who has been and is making herself ready. You are my beloved and I am Yours. I linger on that one sentence. You are mine and I am Yours (Song of Sol. 6:3 paraphrased). What does that mean amid a dying and perverse generation? Can that one declaration change things and make a difference? I say, "Yes."

2. I come with a made-up mind, entering this day. I will not be persuaded by what I see or hear. I will allow You, the champion of my soul, to rule and reign. I will not give in, go back or cease the momentum of living for the King of Kings. I have chosen You, and You have chosen me. In that moment of time, I was changed forever. Now I live a life for You and You alone.

3. You have preeminence in my thoughts and deeds, in words and actions. I declare it to the north, south, east, and west. I live for You. Every power and principality must eventually bow to You, **so why not now**? My goal is to see it happen wherever I am and wherever I go. The enemy understands I belong to You and You alone. So, I begin the day with prayer; I enter Your courts with thanksgiving. I come into Your gates with praise (Ps. 100:4 paraphrased). Even now, I declare that this is the day You have made. My choice is this: I will rejoice and be glad in it (Ps. 118:24 paraphrased).

4. Yes, this is taking place because of You. You are my beloved and I am Yours. I go through the day with Your banner of love over me. Even

when times are difficult, I touch this banner, and I can sense Your presence. It is real and tangible. It is the love of the Bridegroom to His bride. I breathe, and it's You. Peace is there. Your peace surrounds me, envelopes me, entwines me...That's what I desire. I choose **You** because You first chose me.

5. I call out to my Groom, "Come into every area of my life." I find joy in You. I find peace in You. I find the manifestation of Your presence. It is in me, near me, and around me. I don't hold back. I corral all my fleshly ways and place them at Your footstool. I take up only that on which You have breathed a holy, *"Yes"*.

6. I will not delay, as I am about the Father's business. I am thankful for this love-relationship and friendship I have with Jesus. Therefore, I know what to do and say. It echoes and mirrors heaven. I won't give into temptation to do it my way or the world's way. The enemy tries to ensnare me, but I declare today: "I will not be tricked nor lulled to sleep. I stand ready!"

7. I have set myself up for success: reading the word, praying the word, fellowshipping with those who are running hard after the things of God, being in church, and allowing myself to be washed with the word. All of this comes together to spell SUCCESS—not in the worldly sense, but in heaven's eyes. I tell my soul, "I will not stop or slow down. I will not give in or give up. I will not allow my flesh to lead." (I declare, decree, and confess this today, in Jesus' name. I command myself to align with that declaration!)

8. I <u>will</u> release Heaven to earth; I <u>will</u> listen and obey; I <u>will</u> feed my spirit man, and it <u>will</u> grow up to its full stature that God ordained before the creation of the world for me. My flesh bows to this and obeys. The training I put myself through is because I have seen how the mighty have fallen, and I declare loudly—"**NOT ME!** You can't have me. *I am making myself ready"* (Rev. 19:7 paraphrased).

9. It is for the marriage of the Lamb. That is my heart's desire and my heart's cry. Hear me! Help me! Join with me! That decree reverberates through the atmosphere. It continues, gathering momentum. Those with the same heart and spiritual DNA come into sync with this prayer, and a resounding "YES" explodes the air, bringing Heaven to earth and the love of the Bridegroom for His bride. That's the plan, and I won't back down until Your kingdom collides with this earthly

kingdom and I see it with my eyes in the land of the living…in the mighty name of Jesus! AMEN and AMEN and AMEN!

What other prayers or thoughts has this prayer evoked from you to the Lord? Write them here.

_____

_____

_____

_____

_____

_____

_____

_____

Journal personal notes, thoughts, prophetic words, and ideas you are hearing or sensing from the Lord. This may even include Scripture He is showing you.

_____

_____

_____

_____

_____

_____

_____

_____

Seventeen
His Paths are Beyond Tracing Out

Dedicated to Tommie and Elaine Hayes, and Dawn Wells

"Oh, the depth of the riches of the wisdom and knowledge of God! How unsearchable his judgments, and his paths beyond tracing out!" (Romans 11:33 NIV).

1. O, Father, I come into agreement with these words today, searching for that which appears, at first glance, unsearchable—Your judgments. My prayer is to join You in tracing paths that are untraceable; to prove to myself and others that even though God's wisdom is to a depth that is unfathomable, You desire for me to obtain it.

2. I am riveted, yet overwhelmed, by the mere thought that You came to earth for me. You died and rose for me. I stand in awe at what Your death, burial, and resurrection bought. You did it that I could be set free from sin and death. Your atoning sacrifice established the covenant that I freely walk in.

3. I am cocooned in Your covenant and love that was established at the cross, given freely by Jesus, sent by Abba, Daddy—the Father. *Yes, Your ways are beyond tracing out* (Romans 11:33 paraphrased). I can barely comprehend that You, my Lord and Savior, would freely choose to do this for me. My faith reaches to grasp this truth, but I am unable to adequately do so. Understanding evades me. Submission is before me; I say, "Yes."

4. You're alive, and I fall into the center of Your provisions. I am a king's kid and Your ambassador, representing You to all. While I enjoy this closeness, I tap into Your riches filled with wisdom and knowledge. I am close enough to breathe in Your presence, and just one moment brings a lifetime of understanding. It overwhelms me, establishing peace in my thinking—wisdom combined with knowledge brings results.

5. I inhale You and exhale all that is not You. My decree is simple, "I give all that I am for Your unsearchable judgments" (Romans 11:33

paraphrased). I command my thoughts, ways, appetites, manners, and customs to align with You, releasing pent-up passion and devotion. The kicking and screaming of my carnal ways align with holiness at the mention of Your name.

6. Understanding comes; but it is not immediate. I have an *a-ha moment* as the Holy Spirit, my Comforter and Teacher, guides me to truth. At the same time, I whisper, "Just one glance…one touch…one moment with You—my King!" This shines Your light and establishes my ways.

7. My prayer and desire is simple—my life devoted to You—set free by Calvary to be all that You called me to be. I speak alignment to myself, family, and _____ (name church) to become all that Your design requires. Destiny is my past, present, and future. I step into Your ways, thoughts, paths, and deeds—those that are beyond tracing out, full of the riches of wisdom and knowledge. I do this declaring, "You are worthy to receive all glory, honor, and praise" …in the mighty name of Jesus. Amen!

What other prayers or thoughts has this prayer evoked from you to the Lord? Write them here.

_____

_____

_____

_____

_____

_____

_____

_____

Journal personal notes, thoughts, prophetic words, and ideas you are hearing or sensing from the Lord. This may even include Scripture He is showing you.

_____

_____

_____

_____

_____

_____

_____

_____

_____

Eighteen
The Lord is My Portion

Dedicated to Joseph Tillman and The Ramp, Hamilton, Alabama

*"The Lord is my portion," says my soul, "therefore I will hope in him"
(Lam. 3:24 ESV).*

1. In the midst of every trial and heartache, I declare to my soul, "The Lord is my portion!" (Therefore I have hope.) I shout to the naysayers, "The Lord is my portion!" (Therefore I have hope.) I decree it to the forces that have set themselves up against me, "The Lord is my portion!" (Therefore I have hope.) This is my just reward, and in this I rest and have peace. Yet, sometimes life is difficult. So please hear my plea for help.

2. Even when things are going smoothly, let my cry be the same, "The Lord is my portion!" Therefore, I **will not**, **cannot**, **do not** fret. I command my emotions to align, and I set my gaze on You, the Author and Finisher of my faith. There is no doubt where my triumph lies—in You and You alone.

3. How magnificent are Your ways toward me. How tremendous are Your thoughts. I can scarcely believe that You are for me and not against me. You have set my feet on solid ground. You have aligned my thoughts. I think on You. I ask for Your help and You say, "Yes!"

4. The King of the Universe—the Most High God displays His beauty for all to see. At times it is seen in the most unlikely place—me. Knowing this gives You pleasure, my request is that You flow through me. Allow others to know You because of what they see in me. Help me to freely give, being about the Father's business. May I realize that it is for one reward—YOU. You are my great reward. You reward me with You—my portion. I breathe, drink, and absorb You into every fiber of my being as I go about my daily business. Yet, I continually give You away. My portion is supernatural and never runs out.

5. May I not look back or dwell on former things that are unimportant for today. May I never take for granted all that You've done and all I've

received. May I allow Your presence to come in such a tangible way that my breath and Yours are in unison; my heart beats in sync with heaven; my mind is in focus with You—my great reward.

6.   What else is there that can compare to the portion I have? What can come close? The answer is easy: no person or anything the world has to offer. So, I stop the comparison. My search leads only to You. Do not allow me to look for love in all the wrong places, nor allow counterfeit portions to appease me. My flesh is weak; yet, in my failings and sufferings, I am still running hard after You. I am still obtaining that imperishable reward; I am still receiving the interest of my portion. How can that be? Selah.

7.   Even in my weakness and as the world condemns me, pouring out penalties for the sins I've committed, You continue to pour and pour into my supernatural bank account. It makes no sense to my mind; it is YOU—my portion—even when I don't deserve it and didn't earn it. Your answer is always the same, "My child, YES, I love you. Yes, I died for you. Yes, I'd do it again. Yes, I am your portion." This truth is difficult to comprehend and even more difficult to receive; therefore, my mind wants to deny it. By faith, I accept it and say, "Thank You!"

8.   Since I can't earn it, please help me to be worthy of all that Your death represents! Help me not take Your love and mercy for granted. Help me be one who says, "Yes," and means it—even when it does not go my way. Today, this is my decision: "**I fret not,** because *You are my portion and great reward* (Lam. 3:24 paraphrased). I receive this in the mighty name of Jesus." Amen.

What other prayers or thoughts has this prayer evoked from you to the Lord? Write them here.

_____

_____

_____

_____

_____

_____

_____

_____

Journal personal notes, thoughts, prophetic words, and ideas you are hearing or sensing from the Lord. This may even include Scripture He is showing you.

_____

_____

_____

_____

_____

_____

_____

_____

_____

Nineteen
I Press

Dedicated to Kathy Elash and my mentoring group, From Called to Chosen

"Not that I have already obtained all this, or have already been made perfect, but I press on to take hold of that for which Christ Jesus took hold of me. Brothers, I do not consider myself yet to have taken hold of it. But one thing I do: Forgetting what is behind and straining toward what is ahead, I press on toward the goal to win the prize for which God has called me heavenward in Christ Jesus" (Phil 3:12-14 NIV).

1. Heavenly Father, I don't claim to be perfect in any way. Yet, I understand that Your word calls me upward to that higher calling in You. I want to obtain that which appears to be unattainable and out of my reach.

2. So, today I declare and decree over my life, I <u>will</u> tap into a heavenly principle...the unknown mystery that can only be described as a **BUT GOD...a suddenly from heaven.** It is not me; it is <u>all</u> You—the living God within. I will not be lackadaisical or lazy; I will PRESS! I won't allow my flesh to rule. I call forth the spirit-man within and press to take hold of that which Jesus took hold of for me on the cross. I allow the finished work to step into my day, and the covenant Your blood bought to transcend my life.

3. I refuse to dwell on past mistakes and failures; instead I take hold of that which YOU took hold of for me. I don't understand this mystery; so I set myself up for victory by simply saying, "Yes," to You and allowing myself to come into agreement with this scripture.

4. I declare, "Old thinking must go." In its place, I allow Your thoughts and presence to encapsulate me. I understand this doesn't happen just because I think it or will it. Instead, day by day...hour by hour...moment by moment, I yield all of me—including my thoughts...ways...desires...abilities—even my appetites!

5. I am Yours in every sense that I can be. I know it may be a long and laborious road; yet, I willingly take the route that You have for me. It is not the path of least resistance. It is not the wide road. It is the narrow path. I choose to forget what is behind. I choose to strain for what You have placed ahead of me.

6. I'm going for broke, pressing and straining toward the goal—YOU. That is also my prize! I am not satisfied until I see, appropriate, realize, and apportion all that You have for me. While I'm on this planet called earth, I continue to strive, to the best of my ability, to serve You, the living God. But, it's for the eternal prize that You have called me to obtain.

7. This is my reality; this is what I desire; this is what I live for. There will be no turning back, no giving up, no yielding to my fleshly ways…I want to live for You, body, soul, and spirit. I want to experience the best me, because I've yielded myself to You. I am in the world, not of the world. My carnal appetites will not rule me, for I know that *greater is He that is in me than he that is in the world* (1John 4:4 paraphrased).

8. My declaration is that *I will press*; *I will receive the prize*. For I know that my victory lies in You—not anything or anyone else! *You are "the way and the truth, and the life"* (John 14:6 NIV). I am yielded to this—my appetites will not win this fleshly battle, because **today** I've chosen to PRESS, in the mighty name of Jesus! Amen!

W hat other prayers or thoughts has this prayer evoked from you to the Lord? Write them here.

_____

_____

_____

_____

_____

_____

_____

J ournal personal notes, thoughts, prophetic words, and ideas you are hearing or sensing from the Lord. This may even include Scripture He is showing you.

_____

_____

_____

_____

_____

_____

_____

_____

Twenty
Cast Your Cares

Dedicated to my First Place 4 Health Class, Newnan, GA

"Cast all your anxiety on him because he cares for you" (1 Peter 5:7 NIV).

"Casting all your care upon him; for he careth for you" (1 Peter 5:7 KJV).

1. Abba, Daddy, I stand amazed at You, casting all my cares upon YOU, for You care for me. I am grateful that as Your child, this is a given—a *done-deal*, so to speak. Therefore, thanksgiving is continually on my lips—the fruit of praise going forth, that You, my King and Lord, are worthy to receive.

2. My shoulders were not meant to carry all the burdens that life brings my way. When I continually take on additional things that You freely desire to handle, it becomes false burden-bearing on my part, opening the door for the enemy to heap more and more on me until I am crushed under the weight of doing it all myself.

3. Today I stop and say, *"No more,"* to every demonic force that has set itself against me. When I've done all I know to do, I stand in faith, knowing that You are dependable in *all things*. I am elated by this and shout praises to You. *"I am the victor, the victim no more!"*

4. My family and church also benefit from this declaration. This sets them upon Your path, going forward as recipients of the "no greater love" Biblical example. You willingly demonstrated this on the cross for all to see. This evokes praise and worship, prayer and thanksgiving over and over and over again. My prayers and songs burst forth as a symphony of worship to the only One worthy enough to receive it.

5. I almost feel like an innocent bystander—a pawn, watching what is taking place, and feeling undone by all You do for me. So I fall at Your feet in speechless adoration and awe—words are inadequate. I have a made-up mind that I won't keep this just for me. My prayer is

that every person I encounter will be a recipient of this magnanimous love and grace. Just one glance, and I am undone in Your presence.

6. Thank You that testimony after testimony comes forth from me because I have chosen to obey this scripture and to the best of my ability have carried only that which You required. The treasure of this scripture is seen in the benefits my children, grandchildren, spouse, and extended family receive daily. Because You carried this punishment in Your body on the cross, and I daily release all anxiety to You, miracles are released from heaven and angels are sent to guard my way.

7. It is a never-ending cycle…I cast my cares upon You… You carry them and release what is needed at the exact perfect time Everyone who comes in contact with me—friends, family, and associates receive the benefits that come from You carrying the cares I cast upon You. It starts again: I cast my cares upon You… You carry them and release what is needed at the exact perfect time. Everyone who comes in contact with me—friends, family, and associates receive the benefits that come from You carrying the cares I cast upon You. *"Oh, what a relief it is!"* …body, soul, and spirit…even my appetite bows in the process. Your ways are so much higher than I can imagine or understand. I give You all praise, glory, and honor due You, in the name of Jesus Christ of Nazareth. Amen and Amen!

What other prayers or thoughts has this prayer evoked from you to the Lord? Write them here.

_____

_____

_____

_____

_____

_____

_____

_____

Journal personal notes, thoughts, prophetic words, and ideas you are hearing or sensing from the Lord. This may even include Scripture He is showing you.

_____

_____

_____

_____

_____

_____

_____

_____

Twenty-one
The Lion of the Tribe of Judah Roars

Dedicated to my Coweta Community Church Family

"Listen! Listen to the roar of his voice, to the rumbling that comes from his mouth. He unleashes his lightning beneath the whole heaven and sends it to the ends of the earth. After that comes the sound of his roar; he thunders with his majestic voice. When his voice resounds, he holds nothing back. God's voice thunders in marvelous ways; he does great things beyond our understanding" (Job 37:2-5 NIV).

"'The Lord will roar from on high; He will thunder from his holy dwelling and roar mightily against his land. He will shout like those who tread the grapes, shout against all who live on the earth. The tumult will resound to the ends of earth, for the Lord will bring charges against the nations; He will bring judgment on all mankind and put the wicked to the sword,'" declares the Lord (Jer. 25:30-31 NIV).

The LORD will roar from Zion and thunder from Jerusalem; the earth and the sky will tremble. But the LORD will be a refuge for his people, a stronghold for the people of Israel (Joel 3:16 NIV).

1.   Heavenly Father, I hear You say, "I Am roaring from heaven. Do you feel it and hear it? Can you see what I'm doing? I Am releasing My roar; will you participate with me?" What can I say but, "Yes." It may be a weak yes, but it is yes indeed.

2.   Allow Your presence to burn within me in such a way that I am overtaken and consumed. Your roar is to get my attention, that of Your bride and remnant. Yet, what does it mean? How do I participate with You? I know it's possible because of the living-ness of Almighty God.

3.   You continually show me a new facet of Yourself; yet You change not. I stand in agreement with You, allowing You to overwhelm and overtake my faculties so that I am out of the way and You are what overshadows me—body, soul, and spirit. I come into alignment with

the heavenly roar, capturing hearts of those in need of salvation, repentance from dead works, and sin that so easily entangles.

4. I will not give up nor give in to the ways of the world that are detrimental to all that You stand for and for which You died. I sense You are holding back the floodgates of judgment, standing ready to relent...*if...and...but...*

5. Your roar is for a heartfelt, genuine repentance. Let it be on the hearts and minds of Your people. Let it resound like trumpets that are sounded before a great announcement.

6. *If my people who are called by my name would humble themselves and turn from their wicked ways* (2 Chron.7:14 paraphrased) ...repenting for their words, actions, and deeds...plus that of their nation. I hear You prophetically say, "Would I not willingly hold back the flashes of lightning that heaven thunders, that bring judgment?" (I know You are a good and gracious God.) Yes! You would!

7. My cry is in unison with heaven. *Your mercies are new every morning* (Lam. 3:23 paraphrased). Show mercy for the sake of Your children and for Your name's sake. I am asking, beseeching, and pleading earnestly. Hear my insistent cry for mercy, peace, and grace. Do not forsake me nor turn Your back. I choose to roar with You. Allow heaven to be released today through Your humble servant. Yes, I roar with You!

8. The despicable practices that have put the angel army on alert have gotten my attention. I am Your soldier; I release the heavenly roar from the depths of my being today in unison with the Lion of the tribe of Judah. I will not go back; I will not stop; I will not relent until I hear the trumpet sound, the sky split, and see the King of Kings return in glory. To the best of my ability, I hold nothing back and release this prayer over myself, my family and my church...in the mighty name of Jesus! Amen!

What other prayers or thoughts has this prayer evoked from you to the Lord? Write them here.

_____

_____

_____

_____

_____

_____

_____

Journal personal notes, thoughts, prophetic words, and ideas you are hearing or sensing from the Lord. This may even include Scripture He is showing you.

_____

_____

_____

_____

_____

_____

_____

_____

Twenty-two
Have You Not Heard?

Dedicated to Rick Watson

"Do you not know? Have you not heard? The LORD is the everlasting God, the Creator of the ends of the earth. He will not grow tired or weary, and his understanding no one can fathom. He gives strength to the weary and increases the power of the weak. Even youths grow tired and weary, and young men stumble and fall; but those who hope in the LORD will renew their strength. They will soar on wings like eagles; they will run and not grow weary, they will walk and not be faint (Isa. 40:28-31 NIV).

1. Heavenly Father, I'm coming in the mighty name of Jesus, bowing down at Your feet to worship You, enthroning You on my heart daily. My utmost and innermost desire is that I would worship You in Spirit and in truth—giving all that I am as an offering to You. Your incredible ways astound me. I know that I know that I know, You have but one goal in mind for me: destiny. This is to advance the Kingdom of God. Your word tells me it is *near me, in me and around me.* (Rom. 10:8 paraphrased). I choose to participate with You, listening intently.

2. *"Do you not know? Have you not heard?"* (Is. 40: 21 NIV), echoes within my spirit-man and that brings a hunger and thirst that only You can satisfy. This is the message I want to shout from the housetops to those who have not heard or have forgotten: ***"The LORD is the everlasting God, the Creator of the ends of the earth"*** (Is. 40:28 NIV). The fullness of this sentence may escape me for a moment; yet, it draws me to You, the lover of my soul. I breathe out. *You don't grow weary* (Is 40:28 paraphrased)—even in the midst of my weariness, trials, and daily routines.

3. You have understanding that I want to comprehend, yet it evades me. So, I trust You for every outcome; I stand in awe of You and how You give me strength when I am weary. In my weakness, You increase my power. You birth through me those things that are on Your heart that

will bring to fruition Your plans that were established *before the creation of the earth.*

4.   I recall this scripture: "I was young and now I am old, yet I have never seen the righteous forsaken or their children begging bread" (Ps. 37:25 NIV). So, I yield myself—body, soul, and spirit, knowing that even *if youths grow tired and weary, and young men stumble and fall* (Is. 40:31 paraphrased), I have a secret weapon: YOU! You're faithful to complete and fulfill Your word. It <u>will not</u>...<u>does not</u>...<u>cannot</u>...go out and return without accomplishing the purposes You have sent it forth to do. (Is. 55:11 paraphrased). This is my belief and confession. I put my hope in You.

5.   I decree and declare that *my strength is renewed* (Is. 40:31 paraphrased and Job 29:20 NLT paraphrased). It is not the typical rejuvenation that one can easily grasp. Rather, it is of Biblical proportions and of a divine nature because of the covenant promises I walk in. Your word states it; I receive it. *I will soar on wings like eagles. I will run and not grow weary; I will walk and not be faint* (Is. 40:31 paraphrased).

6.   This is not only my hope, but my declaration. I don't merely state it; I attach my faith to these words. I follow the pattern of the eagle. I forsake my natural, carnal, earthly ways and catch the wind of the Spirit. My soaring can only take place as my faith captures the will of God, and I let go.

7.   Help me today and allow me to ride the waves of Your Spirit—Your will be done. Help me to stop working in my strength, and instead, yield myself to You. Then and only then will I possess this supernatural strength that allows me not to grow weary or faint. My natural inclination is to want to be in control; but instead I yield that to You. My prayer and desire is that my strength, thoughts, ways, attitudes, deeds, and ideas would be You, extending through me to all that I encounter.

8.   I yield myself daily and receive the fresh oil of anointing. This takes me above my problems and carnal ways. I soar on the atmospheric thermals of Almighty God and proclaim to powers and principalities that I will obey all that the Lord has for me. My goal and desire is yielded to the point that I can say, "Yes, I do know! And yes, I have heard!" It is not me but rather You, and all of this is in the mighty name of Jesus. Amen.

W hat other prayers or thoughts has this prayer evoked from you to the Lord? Write them here.

_____

_____

_____

_____

_____

_____

_____

_____

J ournal personal notes, thoughts, prophetic words, and ideas you are hearing or sensing from the Lord. This may even include Scripture He is showing you.

_____

_____

_____

_____

_____

_____

_____

_____

Twenty-three
Hearts Fully Committed to YOU

Dedicated to Naphtali and Frank Seamster

"For the eyes of the LORD range throughout the earth to strengthen those whose hearts are fully committed to him" (2 Chron. 16:9 NIV).

"For the eyes of the LORD run to and fro throughout the whole earth, to shew himself strong in the behalf of them whose heart is perfect toward him" (2 Chron. 16:9 KJV).

1. Today, I stop, pause, and meditate on this one thing: *for the eyes of the LORD range throughout the earth to strengthen those whose hearts are fully committed (perfect) to/toward him* (2 Chron. 16:9 paraphrased). Is it even possible for me to claim this as a truth in my life? Yet, this is my aim. God is my target.

2. I prayerfully release these questions. How can I get more of YOU? More of Your strength? More of Your power? There is but one way…to live a life that is fully devoted to You. I release this thought in prayer today. Help me, Lord. Help me go to the next level of devotion to You—no longer just words spoken from this love-sick child, but I want those who look at my life to read it like an autobiography written to please the King of Kings.

3. So today, I'm calling on You to show me what I must do. Teach me how to love You rightly…to love You well…to love You the way that pleases You. Teach me how to serve You in all areas of my life. When I have been weak and superficial, teach me how to be powerful and profound as a pursuer of God's holiness and righteousness. I want to be one that captures the heart and eyes of the Lord.

4. I know that Your eyes are on the sparrow…they're also on me. Yet I want to capture that one glance of Your eyes that shows that You know You're the *lover of my soul,* and I'm a sold-out soldier in the army of God. As You search and indwell me, please, Lord, show Yourself strong on my behalf…a mortal whose heart yearns to be

perfect toward You. Is that even possible? I don't know; yet, that is my longing, the very desire of my heart, and the essence of who I am.

5.   I was created to be a God-chaser...a God-pleaser...one who runs hard after You to Shift the Spiritual Atmosphere of my life, (name your church) _____ and this world. I choose not to grow weary in well-doing. I choose to acknowledge You in all my ways; then You will direct my path. Thank You for directing it to that timeless place in the spirit where there is no doubt that I am committed and devoted to one thing—YOU!

6.   I live, eat, and breathe for God alone. This is my declaration; I shout it for all to hear, "You are *my Beloved and I am* Yours." (Song of Songs 6:3 paraphrased). To some this may sound crazy; but my quest is to allow this devotion to make a statement. Let this statement be my prayer. Take this prayer and transform me into who You say that I am.

7.   I will not back down; I will not stop; I will not allow the enemy of my soul and my flesh to win. I will allow God into my life more fully than ever. You alone are my heart's desire. *Your ways are beyond tracing out* (Rom. 11:33 paraphrased). Your thoughts toward me are as vast as the ocean. Your love is higher than the sky. I have captured that one glance. It has left me undone in Your presence and longing for more of You.

8.   Yet I don't stop; I desire another glance...another touch...another insight of knowing. I must have more of YOU. I am addicted to Your presence. One touch leaves me longing for the next. "More" is the cry of my heart. Hear me. Change me. Help me. Encourage me. Strengthen me. I want to be fully devoted/committed/perfect toward You. This is my prayer, in the name of Jesus, my Savior and Lord. Amen.

What other prayers or thoughts has this prayer evoked from you to the Lord? Write them here.

_____

_____

_____

_____

_____

_____

_____

_____

Journal personal notes, thoughts, prophetic words, and ideas you are hearing or sensing from the Lord. This may even include Scripture He is showing you.

_____

_____

_____

_____

_____

_____

_____

_____

Twenty-four
The Breaker Anointing

Dedicated to the women of the Pathway House, Newnan, Georgia

"One who breaks open the way will go up before them; they will break through the gate and go out. Their king will pass through before them, the LORD at their head" (Micah 2:13 NIV).

"The breaker goes up before them; They break out, pass through the gate and go out by it. So their king goes on before them, And the LORD at their head" (Micah 2:13 NASU).

"The breaker is come up before them: they have broken up, and have passed through the gate, and are gone out by it: and their king shall pass before them, and the LORD on the head of them" (Micah 2:13 KJV).

1. *"Let God arise; Let His enemies be scattered"* (Ps. 68:1 NKJV). Let the trumpet sound and heaven's culture come to earth. Let the King of Glory arise that all may know that there is only one true and faithful God—the Lord Almighty...*the One who was and is and is to come!*

2. **You** are the maker of heaven and earth. **You** are the one that finds good pleasure in all that *seek first the Kingdom of God.* So, that is what I do. I seek You with my whole heart...my whole mind...my whole soul and being. Let it be a pleasing aroma to You—the One who sits upon the throne. Let it capture Your heart and attention. Let it release the anointing that breaks through and stops the delay.

3. I cry out, "Come as the Breaker—release the break-through. Come as One who crashes demonic walls, breaks through the enemy's gate, removes Satan's obstacles and crushes every force that stands in Your way!"

4. Wanting Your timing and alignment, I declare, "Your will...not my will be done." I stand ready to be a vessel that You can flow through to others. I pray for all walls around my heart to be removed, in the name of Jesus. This allows Your presence to overwhelm every

obstruction. I'm asking, "Would You surround my heart with Your hands so that I never close You and others out due to hurt and pain? Would You envelop it so that this is no longer an option?" My goal is an unencumbered heart—free to hear and see You more clearly; it allows me to flow with You, and my heart to beat in sync with the Lover of my soul—my Bridegroom.

5. This breaker anointing allows me to see the captives set free and alignment take place everywhere the Lord calls me to go and to everyone He calls me to comfort with prayer, deliverance, and ministry. It is not me; it is the Holy Spirit within. I'm a vessel who has said, "Yes." This aligns me with heaven, releasing God to flow through me. This makes me shout, sing, dance, proclaim, and pray about the glorious excellency of my God.

6. My prayer goes forth, "Let none stand in the way of Your will being done; let the forces that may trample the majesty of my King be thwarted; let those who oppose step aside so that the King of Glory may come in, sup with me, and God's will be further established today." No going back. "Advance…advance…advance" is my cry.

7. Do not allow the dawdling of my soul to slow me down or impede the forward momentum. I speak to my soul, commanding it to get serious and not allow distractions to be a hindrance. "My God is an awesome God" sings forth from my mouth as Your ways are established in me, my family, (name your church) _____, this area, and nation.

8. My heart longs and cries out for the breaker anointing that leads to break-through, alignment, and freedom. I trust You for a magnitude that results in changed lives, sold out to You one hundred percent, leading to revival. It must be in Your time, revival that lasts and transforms an area that affects a nation. Why not, Lord? Use me…use me…use me…that's my plea; that's my prayer; that's my purpose in life.

9. I bind up delay and declare, "I will not stop until the Lord says, '*Well done My good and faithful servant* (Matt. 25:21 paraphrased). *Enter into your rest*'" (Matt. 25:34 paraphrased). Then, I will know that I know. You have heard me, and destiny has been fulfilled. This is my cry from the depths of my being, in the mighty name of Jesus. Amen!

What other prayers or thoughts has this prayer evoked from you to the Lord? Write them here.

_____

_____

_____

_____

_____

_____

_____

Journal personal notes, thoughts, prophetic words, and ideas you are hearing or sensing from the Lord. This may even include Scripture He is showing you.

_____

_____

_____

_____

_____

_____

_____

_____

Twenty-five
Releasing the More

Dedicated to Sondra Gaddy

"Blessed are those who hunger and thirst for righteousness, for they will be filled" (Matt. 5:6 NIV).

1. ***"I am not satisfied, Lord! Hear my cry today for 'MORE'! There has to be more and I must have it!"*** This is my heart-felt cry from all my yesterdays, today, and until my plea breaks through to heaven.

I will P-U-S-H:

Pray Until Something Happens!

When will it fully ascend and arrive at the throne room of God? Will it reach the ears of the One for whom my heart longs?

2. I will not give up until it does, and I participate in ***the more*** in the land of the living with all my being. Until then, allow my longing to become insatiable. Allow the desperation of my heart and soul to be such that it releases action on my part—not only a crying out night and day…day and night, until You release MORE into the earth, but also until it becomes my reality—my way of life.

3. May this prayer open heaven's gate and release angelic activity to do what I've dreamed about, but have been unable to obtain. I am thirsty; I am hungry. But it's not a natural thirst or hunger. It is supernatural and can only be quenched by You, Jesus, King of Kings and Lord of Lords. You are the One for whom my heart longs. You are the one whom I long to please. So daily I seek Your face and pursue You.

4. I am reminded of a scripture written so long ago, but a word in season for me ***today***. *"But when he, the Spirit of truth, comes, he will guide you into all truth. He will not speak on his own; he will speak only what he hears, and he will tell you what is yet to come. He will bring glory to me by taking from what is mine and making it known to you. All that belongs to the Father is mine. That is why I said the Spirit will*

take from what is mine and make it known to you" (John 16:13-15 NIV).

5. "Yes, Lord, yes. Teach me, Lord, to work alongside the Holy Spirit, as He guides me into all truth. Teach me to tap into what You're doing and bring heaven to earth. I am Your vessel. Use me to bring glory to You. Help me, I pray. Help me; I need Your help!"

6. I am also reminded that You spoke of *GREATER... "I tell you the truth, anyone who has faith in me will do what I have been doing. He will do even greater things than these, because I am going to the Father. And I will do whatever you ask in my name, so that the Son may bring glory to the Father. You may ask me for anything in my name, and I will do it"* (John 14:12-14 NIV).

7. Lord, You know what's in my heart. You put it there. My heart burns for the *greater*. This longing keeps me awake at night. My plea is for You to use me. I am no longer interested in being a by-stander. I must see, taste, feel, and experience *the more*. This hooks me into *the greater*. (I'm pleading for this in Your name...)

8. This increases my yearning to be holy—a vessel You desire to flow through. I crave to be at Your side, an extension of You in this world to the lost and dying, to those who need salvation, prayer, healing, prophetic ministry, and deliverance. I know it's not only at hand, but it's available in the here and now. I long to step into it every moment of every day.

9. I believe, declare, and profess, "Wherever I go, things change and shift because of *the more* and *greater* anointing that resides in me, on me, and around me." It's the kingdom of God being advanced through me. I declare to my natural man, "Laziness, pride, unforgiveness, anger, disobedience, and fear must go." I no longer allow these to reside in my temple; there is no room for them or lackadaisical, self-promoting attitudes. I establish singleness of mind and spirit. The focus is You.

10. *The more* is here for me. I must step into it. *It's out with the old; in with the new.* I stand in awe of You and say, "Thank You." Those words seem so hollow and I wonder, who am I that You would be mindful of me? The answer is simple. I am a King's kid. You heard my cry for *more,* and I will never be the same! What an awesome God

I serve. *"I won't let You down."* That's my declaration, and it's in Your mighty name, Jesus, I pray. Amen.

What other prayers or thoughts has this prayer evoked from you to the Lord? Write them here.

_____

_____

_____

_____

_____

_____

_____

_____

Journal personal notes, thoughts, prophetic words, and ideas you are hearing or sensing from the Lord. This may even include Scripture He is showing you.

_____

_____

_____

_____

_____

_____

_____

_____

Twenty-six
Overcoming the Lust of the Flesh and the Pride of Life

Dedicated to Darleen Lindley

"Love not the world, neither the things that are in the world. If any man love the world, the love of the Father is not in him. For all that is in the world, the lust of the flesh, and the lust of the eyes, and the pride of life, is not of the Father, but is of the world" (1 John 2:15-16 KJV).

"But he said to me, 'My grace is sufficient for you, for my power is made perfect in weakness.' Therefore, I will boast all the more gladly about my weaknesses, so that Christ's power may rest on me. That is why, for Christ's sake, I delight in weaknesses, in insults, in hardships, in persecutions, in difficulties. For when I am weak, then I am strong" (2 Corinthians 12:9-10 NIV).

1. Father, I come in the name of Jesus to confess that I am a sinner, saved by grace. The enemy would like me to forget about the saving grace of the cross and keep me in a place of constant turmoil with little or no visible growth. Yet, this grace catapults me to be what and who You declare I am in every situation. It is not grace to do **whatever** I feel like doing; it is grace to go higher and deeper in You…to depart from my natural inclinations and to walk with You as I go through life.

2. I declare today, "I am Your child." The enemy may assail me, knowing my weaknesses. But Your strength keeps me and stabilizes me. It holds me and adjusts me when I need it most. Therefore, I boast in You and You alone. *For you created my inmost being; you knit me together in my mother's womb. I praise you because I am fearfully and wonderfully made; your works are wonderful, I know that full well* (Ps. 139:13–14 NIV).

3. Yet, I gaze upon the invisible shortcomings of my inmost being that stand out to me, which I (wrongly) imagine the world sees. This works to magnify my need for You. Even though I believe that *"I am fearfully and wonderfully made"* (Ps. 139:14 NIV) *and also the*

93

"righteousness of God" (2 Cor. 5:21 NIV) in Christ Jesus, I cry, *"Help my unbelief!"* (Mark 9:24 NKJV) This opens my eyes to only one possible conclusion: my need for You is great.

4. In my mind, I understand that You hold first place and are the Lover of my Soul. You are my Bridegroom and soon-coming King. I am Your bride. Then, why do my thoughts and actions betray what I know to be true? Why do I so easily abandon my First Love? Knowing this, I call upon Your name. You bring comfort, joy, hope, grace, healing, love, and peace.

5. You help me make right choices *to do the next right thing.* You remind me of my righteous standing, purchased with Your blood. You remain my hope! I know the plans of the enemy. He comes to *rob, steal, kill, and destroy* (John 10:10 paraphrased). It plays out in many ways: often as *lust of the flesh, lust of the eyes, and the pride of life* (1 John 2:16 paraphrased). Lust—*a powerful force that produces an intense wanting for an object or circumstance fulfilling the soul...* **but** for a moment! In the end, I am left empty, ashamed, and feeling guilty.

6. I declare, ***"I am a Christian"***—a little Christ. Those things that produce an ungodly lust will never fill the void that can only be filled by YOU. If I hesitate for a moment, it sweeps in with its pledge of desires fulfilled—but gives only empty, hollow, shallow promises...causing this unwanted appetite to overtake me. I know *my spirit is willing* to do what is right, *but my flesh is weak* (Mark 14:38).

7. So today, amid every ungodly ambition that wants to allure and captivate me with its enticing ways, I shout loudly to the King of Kings, repeating the promises that bring life, *"Your grace is sufficient for me, for Your power is made perfect in my weakness!"* (2Cor. 12:9 paraphrased). I speak to my flesh and command it to align with Your word once again.

8. I breathe in Your promises. They get through to my heart and once again bring me the peace that I need for this moment in time. Every breath I breathe is for You. I continue to pray, seek, ask, declare, and yield myself to the One who turns my weaknesses into worship and my slip-ups into strength! This is all for Your glory, honor and praise, in Jesus' name. Amen!

What other prayers or thoughts has this prayer evoked from you to the Lord? Write them here.

_____

_____

_____

_____

_____

_____

Journal personal notes, thoughts, prophetic words, and ideas you are hearing or sensing from the Lord. This may even include Scripture He is showing you.

_____

_____

_____

_____

_____

_____

_____

Twenty-seven
Jesus has Overcome the World

Dedicated to Noreen Holcomb

"I have told you these things, so that in me you may have peace. In this world you will have trouble. But take heart! I have overcome the world" (John 16:33 NIV).

"In this you greatly rejoice, though now for a little while you may have had to suffer grief in all kinds of trials. These have come so that your faith — of greater worth than gold, which perishes even though refined by fire — may be proved genuine and may result in praise, glory and honor when Jesus Christ is revealed" (1 Peter 1:5-7 NIV).

1. *"The name of the Lord is a strong tower; the righteous run in and they are safe"* (Pr. 18:10 NIV). This scripture song goes over and over in my mind and causes me to run into Your arms of love, reminding me there is only ONE who can save (save, heal, and deliver) to the uttermost. You alone are _MY_ strong tower—able to help me in times of need and suffering.

2. During trials and tribulation, I declare Your word: *You turn my mourning into dancing (Ps. 30:22 KJV).* It's a mystery; I don't know how You do it. Yet I don't look for an explanation. I simply trust You and thank You for hiding me in the shadow of Your wings. During seasons of suffering, I have learned to *surrender* all to You. "Take from me everything that is not worthy of YOU," I pray. "Allow what delights **You** to come forth from me during these times as sweet smelling incense. Take me and mold me. Shape me into Your image. *I am Yours; I am Yours,*" is the cry that comes forth from my lips.

3. When trials and temptations result in pain, torment, and affliction, I long to touch You and experience the beauty of Your holiness, gaze upon Your loveliness, and taste Your amazing grace. My plea resounds, "Don't let the heavens be as brass, preventing my prayers from ascending to the throne room of God." I repent and forgive quickly so my prayers are unhindered.

4. Who is like You? The answer is simple, yet more complex than my thoughts can fathom or understand. Even so, *I know that I know* that Your love is abundantly available to me. In a moment of time beyond my comprehension, You allow me to tangibly assimilate this into my spirit-man and at the same time forbid the enemy to take me captive or release unspeakable condemnation upon me. I remain secure and invisible from him...in a hidden place, under the shadow of Your wings (Ps. 91:4 paraphrased).

5. I will not give up until I see You move on my behalf in the land of the living. Though my body may be frail; my spirit soars on wings of eagles and I release this prayer. "Help me O Lord; *my spirit is willing; but my flesh is weak*" (Mark 14: 38 paraphrased). I hear You clearly, "Don't allow any suffering to be wasted; allow it to have its perfect way so that eternal purposes may be worked out."

6. During this, I know You are refining me like gold. You remind me that You have not only overcome the world, but have brought me peace— even when troubles, trials, and sufferings come my way as a part of life. But You never give up on me, and this makes me smile. I am sure my *faith is being proved genuine and **will** result in praise, glory and honor when Jesus Christ is revealed* (1 Pt. 5:7 paraphrased). How can this be? I don't know, yet I love to meditate on it...Your will be done in the mighty name of Jesus. Amen!

What other prayers or thoughts has this prayer evoked from you to the Lord? Write them here.

_____

_____

_____

_____

_____

_____

_____

_____

Journal personal notes, thoughts, prophetic words, and ideas you are hearing or sensing from the Lord. This may even include Scripture He is showing you.

Twenty-eight
Come up Higher, My Beloved

Dedicated to the Mountain Movers Prayer Group

"My beloved is mine, and I am his..." (Song of Sol. 2:16 KJV).

"Can you fathom the mysteries of God? Can you probe the limits of the Almighty? They are higher than the heavens — what can you do? They are deeper than the depths of the grave — what can you know?" (Job 11:7-8 NIV).

"He who descended is the very one who ascended higher than all the heavens..." (Eph. 4:10 NIV).

The following is a prophetic word from the Lord, given to me for the Mountain Movers Prophetic Prayer Group, upon which this prayer is based. Please note, to the best of my ability, the wording and grammar is exactly as spoken to me by the Lord.

> *"God is seated on the throne...higher than any—more than your imagination can take you...farther than the eye can see. Eye has not seen nor has ear heard that which God has planned for His beloved—His bride. It is a time of going higher and deeper—wider and farther. Who can fathom the unfathomable? Who can understand the ways of our King? His love is unlimited; His ways are boundless without measure. This uncreated, indescribable, un-comprehensible God has come and involves you in His affairs. He bids you, 'Come up higher, my beloved. Come up where I take your breath away. Breathe in Me and I will show you things that not many have ever tempted to know or see. Come up higher, my beloved.'"*

1. Heavenly Father, I come to You in the mighty name of Jesus, undone by this one thought, "I am Your beloved; You are mine, and You bid me to 'come higher'." How awesome are Your thoughts and ways

toward me. How incredible it is to come into Your presence. I do so with thanksgiving and praise. I worship and adore You, the One True Living God. There is none like You.

2. Your presence permeates my thoughts, ways, and being. I declare from every fiber of my being, with all that I am, "You are mine, and I am Yours!" There is none like You. I want to see You…to know You…to hear You—today and every day, in the land of the living. I want to go higher and deeper in You. I long to experience the vastness of Your presence. What does this look like, feel like… to know that which is incomprehensible? Allow me for a moment to gaze upon Your loveliness and sense Your goodness and grace. It is too magnificent for words. How I long for You.

3. My heart beats fast at this mere thought. The One who calls me to come higher is the King of Kings and Lord of Lords. Your love for me is more than I can handle, and can't be understood in just one lifetime. Your delight for me, a mere mortal, leaves me undone and shaking my head. I stand in awe of You. I am overwhelmed—a lovesick child who has eyes only for You—my Bridegroom.

4. I try to fathom what all this means, but it is impossible. I know that *when I see You, I will be like You* (1John 3:2 paraphrased). I long for that day, and at the same time I tremble at the mere thought of it. I want to go deeper with You. Will You help me? Will You teach me? Will You lead me? I want to be in sync with You. Each beat of Your heart; each step You take, I want to align with You, observing the blueprint You have for me and walking it out with You, bringing heaven to earth…every step…every breath…every moment of every day!

5. Is this even possible? Is destiny even within my reach? I believe it is. I pray it, declare it, decree it, receive it, and walk in it. Your plan… Your will… Your angels released on my behalf so I can perform the very thing that I was created for, and that which You placed in my heart to do and be. I am part of the Esther generation, and I live *for such a time as this* (Esther 4:14 paraphrased). Do not shield me from what lies ahead; I am Your design, and all that You created *is good* (Gen. 1:31 paraphrased).

6. These are Your intentions inside of me…whispered, spoken, and shouted. Heaven is in my heart, and I release it to the four corners of

the earth as I pray Your will over me, my family, church, and this nation. I don't give up or back down. Destiny is within reach. I will not stop or look back. I look forward to the day when You say, *" 'Well done,'* (Matt. 25: 23 NIV) *My beloved—My bride; enter into your rest. The best is yet to come."*

7. My heart aligns with this, and I hear You speak, "Fear not; you are in My hands; I will never leave you nor forsake you." (Deut. 31: 6 paraphrased). I trust You and believe it.

8. With just one glance You have left me undone. I come to You; the veil has been rent. I come in because I can. You made the way. It was by Your blood. May I never get used to this fact, and may I never take for granted what Your blood did for me. It is still active and alive. One decision to say, "Yes," has changed the course of my history. *I was bought with a price (1 Cor. 6:20 paraphrased). I am not my own.* For this and so much more, I am forever thankful. I give all that I am to You in the mighty name of Jesus. Take me higher. Amen.

W hat other prayers or thoughts has this prayer evoked from you to the Lord? Write them here.

_____

_____

_____

_____

_____

_____

_____

_____

Journal personal notes, thoughts, prophetic words, and ideas you are hearing or sensing from the Lord. This may even include Scripture He is showing you.

_____

_____

_____

_____

_____

_____

_____

_____

_____

Twenty-nine
All In

Dedicated to Michele White, Tina Watson, Jan Colver, and Pamela Hill Tarlton

"Draw near to God and he will draw near to you" (James 4:8 NKJV).

"And whatever you do, whether in word or deed, do it all in the name of the Lord Jesus, giving thanks to God the Father through him" (Col. 3:17 NIV).

1. Holy Spirit, come as my comforter and the one who teaches and guides me into all truth. Forgive me, Lord, for not allowing the Holy Spirit to have His way One hundred percent of the time. Forgive me for thinking more highly of myself than I ought. Forgive me for not allowing Your ways to encompass me all the time.

2. I'm **_all in_** because You're an **_all-in_** God. I don't want to do this thing termed Christianity halfway or halfheartedly. I don't want to lose sight of You at any time. I want Your ways to be my ways.

3. Let it be such that nobody can see where You start and end and where I start and end. Please, Lord, hear my plea today. I cry out for help! Can You hear me? Will You touch me? Will You teach me? Will You contend for me?

4. Allow Your breath to breathe through every pore of my being. I am desperate for You. I'm lost without You. I can fathom no other way of life. I live, eat, and breathe You. I move to the movement of Your thoughts…Your whisper…Your voice. My goal is YOU—to be in sync with You. Let the waves of Your presence hit me and fill me. I long for You: "More, Lord, more!"

5. Even now, I hear the sounds of heaven as the trumpet signals the announcing and beckoning to me—Your bride. You are calling me to come hither. You've heard my cries of desperation and You're sounding the trumpet, announcing Your decrees for me. (I question, "What does this mean?")

6. Then I hear the breaking of glass. You're breaking off all the false ideas and ideals that have kept me from a true encounter with You— the living and One True God. It is these false ideas and facades that have kept me from getting closer and closer to You and others. (Help me lay them at Your footstool.)

7. Today is the day that I choose to do all in Your name and for Your glory. I declare that breakthrough is coming forth; the breaking of old habits, ways, thinking and ideas. These no longer impede my relationship with You nor the destiny You have set before me. Thank You for the sounds of heaven that are breaking forth to accomplish Your will to bring heaven to earth and shift the atmosphere around me, my family, _____ (name your church and area).

8. This is the day that I choose to draw even nearer than I ever have before. As I draw near to You, You draw near to me. Nothing could be sweeter at this moment in time. Thank You for Your divine presence that inhabits and surrounds me. I stand in awe of You as the sounds of heaven resound around me, for Your glory. In the name of Jesus. Amen.

What other prayers or thoughts has this prayer evoked from you to the Lord? Write them here.

_____

_____

_____

_____

_____

_____

_____

_____

J ournal personal notes, thoughts, prophetic words, and ideas you are hearing or sensing from the Lord. This may even include Scripture He is showing you.

_____

_____

_____

_____

_____

_____

_____

_____

Thirty
Kisses of Your Lips

Dedicated to Pete Mullins

Let him kiss me with the kisses of his mouth — for your love is more delightful than wine. Pleasing is the fragrance of your perfumes; your name is like perfume poured out. No wonder the maidens love you! Take me away with you — let us hurry! Let the king bring me into his chambers. We rejoice and delight in you; we will praise your love more than wine. How right they are to adore you!" (Song of Songs 1:2-4 NIV).

1. How I long for You today; whether in this extremely dry and thirsty land—or even in the land of plentiful. How I never want to depart from the delight that the mere thought of You brings me. Therefore, I come into agreement with Your word, and I long to taste that which only You can bestow upon me—the kisses of Your lips.

2. What does it taste like, feel like, smell like? What is it that makes Your kisses more delightful than wine, a fragrance like perfume? It is the unknown factor in the equation of life. It is You and You alone…the triune God upon a mere human vessel, who comes without words, but with love that emanates through every pore of my being. It is a closeness that can't be bought or sold. It can only be given by the Holy One of Israel; it can only be received by Your lovesick child who seeks You above all else.

3. Let me be the maiden—the bride, that goes after You with all that I am. I cry out, "Let it be me! Take me with You. Let me hurry away with You to Your chambers. I want to rejoice and delight in You even more than I ever have. I want to praise and love You more and more. I adore You."

4. Let my adoration play out before You, my King, in inexplicable ways. Let my imagination be purified and sanctified by the touch of the Master's hands. Let me be the one who runs with You, receives the power from on High, and does mighty exploits with You. Let it be me.

5. I never want to grow weary in well doing, but in all my ways let me seek You first. Then I know You will direct my path. Let me be the one who is holy, pleasing, and undefiled—fit for a King. This is my heart; this is my cry: "Let You and me run together, arm-in-arm, hand-in-hand, never separated—doing those things that You created me to do—those things that can only come about or be realized because I have been *kissed by the kisses of Your mouth*." (Song of Songs 1:2 paraphrased).

6. The breath of God flows in me and through me. It engulfs me and circulates around me like a whirlwind. I am no longer my own; I fulfill, to the fullest capacity, that for which You created me to be and do. I don't stop until my destiny is fulfilled, and I hear You say, "'*Well done good and faithful servant*' (Matt. 25:23 NIV). You have reached your destiny. '*Enter into your rest*.'"

7. With just one kiss, one breath, and one moment with the King, I am changed forever. Nothing will ever be the same. How I love You more each day. Let me not fail to give of myself to You. Allow this holy kiss to cause me to transcend who I am to become who You say I am. How I love You and long for You, my most holy and precious Lord. In Jesus' name I pray. Amen.

W hat other prayers or thoughts has this prayer evoked from you to the Lord? Write them here.

_____

_____

_____

_____

_____

_____

_____

_____

Journal personal notes, thoughts, prophetic words, and ideas you are hearing or sensing from the Lord. This may even include Scripture He is showing you.

_____

_____

_____

_____

_____

_____

_____

_____

_____

Shifting the Spiritual Atmosphere

30 Prayers ❋ 30 Days ❋ 30 Minutes

Part II

Group Prayers

These prayers are designed to be spoken boldly, out loud and in a declarative manner. It is recommended that each prayer be personalized for the individual/couple/group that is praying. Be aware that God will inspire you to add whatever is on HIS heart for that specific time.

One
Completing the Work He Began

Dedicated to Steve and Charlotte Rutherford

"...being confident of this, that he who began a good work in you will carry it on to completion until the day of Christ Jesus" (Philippians 1:6 NIV).

1. *In this world there may be trouble, but be of good cheer; I have overcome the world* (John 16:33 paraphrased). In all this overcoming, there we stand in the midst of it...knowing that the good work You began in us will continue until it is completed. How our hearts yearn for this. How we adore You with these thoughts: "Don't stop until You've completed the work. Don't allow the enemy to take us prematurely, before our time. Don't allow the continual wooing of the world and its ways to take the place of our longing for this completion to be accomplished."

2. We know that *You*, our Lord, *will never leave us nor forsake us* (Deut. 31:6 paraphrased). Yet, we see how Godly men and women have backslidden, and that makes us quake at the mere thought of it. We would rather tremble with the touch of Your hand, releasing us to our next assignments—the very thing we were created for.

3. How can we continue a moment longer without that reassurance? Yet, it is before us. The word of God has seared it in our brains; therefore, we continue to remain confident. *He who began a good work in us will not stop until it is completed* (Phil. 1:6 paraphrased). That thought brings us such comfort and overwhelms us to no end.

4. We know to him who has been given much, much is required (Luke 12:48 paraphrased). Once again, we bow our hearts to the One and only—the King of Kings and Lord of Lords. We will not stop short of what You want of us. We will not allow our minds to become engaged otherwise.

5. We will continue to yield every thought, action, and deed to You and You alone. Take this offering and sanctify it, we pray. Take what You

have given us; multiply it; bless it exponentially, and turn it into Your likeness. We don't want to adore You from afar any longer. We want Your majesty to overwhelm us and You alone to be enthroned in our hearts. We adore You.

6. We invite You to come forth and overwhelm us once again. Just one touch...one breath...one moment, and we will be never the same. Today we contend for that. We don't stop short. We contend also for that which You bought for us on the cross. We want to walk in the finished work. We want every drop of Your blood to be utilized to the fullest—nothing wasted.

7. Teach us Lord. We believe we can have it all. You give it freely to those who ask. You said that we could ask, seek, and find (Matt. 7:7 paraphrased). That is what we're doing today. We're asking. *(Do You hear us calling for more?)* We're seeking. *(Can You feel our desperation?)* Our goal is to find You and experience all of You that we can. We want it NOW—in the land of the living. We know it is possible. Teach us. Then, we will teach others. We will not hoard it to ourselves.

8. Let us live a life that pleases You, our King, and these things that You have placed in our hearts will become a reality—not just a prayer, a wish, a hope, or a dream. Circumcise our hearts to all that You have for us.

9. For the Word says—and we believe this for us, *He who began a good work will complete it* (Phil. 1:6 paraphrased). This is what we long for. This is what we ask. Help us rid ourselves of the dross of our lives and receive You in all Your fullness to the absolute glory of God. Allow this request to resound in heaven as others join with us to become who God created each to be before the creation of the world, in Jesus' holy and precious name, Amen and amen.

Two
Releasing the Secret Weapon ~ Righteous Anger

Dedicated to Craig, Lynn, and Jonathan Black and to all who stand up for righteousness when wickedness abounds

"My dear brothers, take note of this: Everyone should be quick to listen, slow to speak and slow to become angry, for man's anger does not bring about the righteous life that God desires" (James 1:19-20 NIV).

"So then, my beloved brethren, let every man be swift to hear, slow to speak, slow to wrath; for the wrath of man does not produce the righteousness of God" (James 1:19-20 NKJV).

"You have knowledge of this, dear brothers. But let every man be quick in hearing, slow in words, slow to get angry; for the righteousness of God does not come about by the wrath of man" (James 1:19-20 BBE).

"Understand this, my dear brothers and sisters: You must all be quick to listen, slow to speak, and slow to get angry. Human anger does not produce the righteousness God desires" (James 1:19-20 NLT).

1. Release it, for the time has come and is now that we must walk void of anger and allow peace which passes all understanding to be the evidence that You live in our hearts and have transformed our lives. Our cry today is that we could rid ourselves of this fleshly anger and wear Your peace like a mantle. Let this mantel cover our minds and shield us from those things that would cause us to stumble.

2. Rid us of malice that would chase us and consume us…bringing bitterness, like bile, into every word we speak and think. We don't want these things; yet, they chase us when we least expect it. We are consumed by it rather than by You and Your presence. We cry out today that Your presence would be like a veil, covering our minds from the tormenter, and that his ways would be far from us. We want

to be *quick to listen;* we desire to be *slow to speak*; but, mostly we yearn to *be slow to anger* (James 1: 19 paraphrased).

3. Hear our confessions; allow these words to penetrate the throne room of God. "We have not been *quick to listen, slow to speak, or slow to anger* (James 1:19 paraphrased). For this and more, we repent." We turn to You, the only One who is able to save to the utmost. With the help of the Holy Spirit, we know You will help us to walk in the righteousness of God.

4. We choose to allow YOU to infiltrate the places that no living person knows about—the deepest, darkest recesses of our souls that even we don't want to look upon. We release them to You, knowing that the cleansing work of the cross will penetrate. It is sufficient! Then and only then will we feel forgiven and free. We can now allow righteous anger to bubble forth.

5. Once You do this cleansing work, we will know it is the Holy Spirit who comes forth in us and not this soulish self that *wants what it wants when it wants it.* Only then can we trust ourselves when we feel the fury and experience the rage. Unrighteous anger and rage is not what we want. Even amid our sins and imperfections, these are the things we long for: that You, our King and Lord, would rule every part of us: body, soul, and spirit.

6. Then, we will shout, cry, call out, and decree things that are pleasing to You—not what our flesh naturally gravitates to and is pleasing to us. Only then will we have the grace and confidence to do as You did, turning over the tables of the moneychangers and allowing righteous indignation and anger to have its proper place in us (Matt. 21:12 paraphrased).

7. Then, we will righteously rage for the lost and abused. Then, we will pray and defend the unborn—those facing abortion and those involved in all sorts of perversion. Then, we will cry out from the deepest depth of our hearts and see You work miracles in this nation once again. Then, we will seek You, and Your face will be before our eyes. We will see that we are changed from glory to glory. How can this be? It's a *"BUT GOD"* moment.

8. As the purity of our prayers reach heaven, we know Your power is released and we are praying what is right <u>and</u> good <u>and</u> pleasing to

You, our Heavenly Father (Deut. 6:18 paraphrased). We want it to be You and not us. That's what we cry out today, releasing anger that is righteous and heavenly decreed, in Jesus' holy, perfect name. Amen.

Three
You Are Our Refuge

Dedicated to Randy and Kim Colver

"In you, O Lord, I have taken refuge; let me never be put to shame. Rescue me and deliver me in your righteousness; turn your ear to me and save me" (Psalms 71:1-2 NIV).

1. Abba, Father, we hear You say, *"Do not let your heart be troubled; neither let it be afraid"* (John 14:27 paraphrased). Even so, today we cry out to You. Hear us and vindicate us, Lord. Do not let the darkness of our souls overtake us. Push it back so all we can see is the light of Your presence. Surround us with Your light.

2. Our ways are full of anguish and we cry out for help; yet no one hears or understands but You. Therefore, we take delight in You. We pour out our hearts before You like a drink offering. The suffering of our souls radiates from us and You alone know. Yet, we take heart because of the same fact: You know.

3. In You and You alone, we take refuge. We hide ourselves in You. We go deeper and deeper knowing that none can find us nor harm us as we lay on Your chest, wrapped in Your love. We stop, stay awhile, and meditate on You and Your covenant promises.

4. Our cries echo forth, "Let our thoughts be pure and of YOU and You alone." The longing for more of You continues forth in a prayer; "Come near to us, O God. Do not forsake us. Allow the richness of Your presence to overtake and overwhelm us."

5. We are thirsty for You. This thing called *life* is dry and we feel forsaken. But, we recall Your promise that *You will never leave us nor forsake us* (Deut. 31:6 paraphrased). Because of this, in the midst of the enemy's attack, we rest knowing *we will never be put to shame* (Ps. 25:3 paraphrased). We meditate on this, even though the frailties of our hearts have a difficult time perceiving it. Our minds apprehend it, knowing You bore that shame on the cross for us. Let this reality be

our reality. Let this truth penetrate until it reaches the uttermost parts of our minds, souls, and spirits. We yield to You. Help us, Lord.

6. We renounce and repent of entertaining spirits of darkness, oppression, depression, fear and dread. We don't want them and send them into the pit, commanding them never to return, in the mighty name of Jesus. We break all their assignments against us as we trust the One who is able to save to the uttermost (Heb. 7:25 paraphrased) and allow You to fill us fuller and fuller. We forsake pain, suffering, anguish, and thought patterns that lead us down this despicable path. We annihilate all this by the Name that's above every name and refuse it to ever return. We turn ourselves over to You—all the way.

7. "Allow the groans within us to burn forth into words that transcend this world into the throne room of God," we shout vehemently! Also, grant us words that are of significant tenderness, yet filled with passion and conviction that the heart of our Abba Daddy takes notice of and is moved by. May they produce such a heavenly stirring that His will is released in us and through us to eradicate all that the enemy has done in sowing seeds of discord and darkness.

8. May Your will strike such a symphony in our hearts that we are now a living, walking, breathing representation of Heaven...only doing, saying, and modeling what we see is taking place by our Heavenly Father. Let this delight transform everything about us. We will not stop until we see our transformation in the land of the living with our eyes. You are God, the Lover of our Soul...the Transformer of our nature...our Bright and Morning Star (Rev. 22:16 paraphrased). All that we need is found in You.

9. We trade our old ways for You. We go forward to reap the benefits sown through this prayer. We find glimmers of joy as the transforming power of Your presence changes us. Our hope is in You and You alone. It overwhelms us and overtakes us. Finally, there is peace all around us. You carry us and we feel loved; You have turned Your ear to us and given solace to our souls. Our salvation overtakes us and we can truly say, *"It is well with our souls."* Thank You, Lord, in the mighty name of Jesus. Amen.

Four
Hearing Your Voice

Dedicated to Amanda Long and Lauren Trogdon

"Whether you turn to the right or to the left, your ears will hear a voice behind you, saying, "This is the way; walk in it (Isaiah 30:21 NIV).

1. Father, today, we come to You in the mighty name of Jesus. Our cries reach to heaven and we are set free more and more—every day, every hour, and every moment to be more of what You want us to be. We will not stop until we reach that thing for which we were created— destiny. We know that before the creation of the earth, You had a plan for our lives. We believe and our mouth declares, *"It is good."*

2. We are about the Father's business. We believe and trust You for the fulfillment of this scripture. We know *whether we turn to the right or to the left,* it makes no difference because we serve an amazing and sovereign God. We hear a voice that leads and directs our paths. We know which way to walk. We hear You. We obey You. Today, we thank You for directing our paths. Our plan is not north, south, east or west; it is the direction of God. You lead and direct our every step through dreams, visions, prophesies, and the Bible...all the time, every day. How awesome You are!

3. The paths of many take them to unknown places that lead to the valley of dry bones (Ez. 37:1 paraphrased). Not us! This is not where we want to be, so we listen to Your voice. We want to be directed every moment, every second, every hour, every day to the places that You have for us. Destiny is calling. Let us not waste one second traveling in the wrong direction and taking up false mantles or counterfeit ways. Pleasing our Savior is what drives us. We are driven by the One and only true God. Day in and day out, we walk in the unknown. Yet, we know it is firmly established and charted by the One who is able to save to the uttermost—our Savior and King!

4. Today, we declare to our ears, "Hearing, come forth in a way that keeps us attuned to the Lord. Senses, activate!" We yield all our senses to You. Would You touch our mouths to declare words that are sweet

yet filled with Heaven—released to the earth? Would You breathe Your breath through us? Would You allow our breath to be so mingled with Yours that a new oneness that we have never experienced before comes forth?

5. We declare this presence is tangible and noticeable, breaking chains of darkness within and without that we did not even know existed. We come into alignment with You and command all our senses to do the same. Daily, we sanctify them over and over again by Your Word and Your presence. Our choice is You! No other will do.

6. Even our touch and smell notice new God fragrances and feel the tangible presence. How can they not when the God of the Universe orchestrates every move with a voice directing our paths? Thank You for sanctified ears that hear Your voice directing us daily. We don't understand how this is all possible, yet, we surrender to You. As we go through the process, we understand more and more. Simultaneously, we care less and less for anything that's not all about You. We yield ourselves to Your will, Your plan, and Your ways.

7. These lovesick children release *"all"* to You—believing, declaring, decreeing, and crying out, "Yes, there is a voice that we can hear that directs us every step of the way." Even past wrongs we've committed and past guilts that want to haunt us surrender to Your ways. We know everything we've ever done has brought us to this time and place. We now understand, with every fiber of our being, that You love us and direct us every inch of the way. Your plan unfolds before our eyes and we continually marvel at it. That which was impossible is now possible! For this we give You all glory, honor, and praise. We pray this in Your precious name...Jesus. Amen, amen, and amen.

Five
Forgiveness

This is for all that have dedicated their lives to being un-offendable in the last days.

"Forgive us our debts, as we also have forgiven our debtors. And lead us not into temptation, but deliver us from the evil one. For if you forgive men when they sin against you, your heavenly Father will also forgive you. But if you do not forgive men their sins, your Father will not forgive your sins" (Matthew 6:12-15 NIV).

1. We yield our hearts to You today. The things that have caused us pain try to light on us and remind us of our past failures. We declare, demanding freedom today, "We don't want this!" So, why are these thoughts here? Why do they remind us of things we don't want to remember? We forgive over and over; yet, our hearts do not seem to align. So, once again, we forgive, knowing this will open the floodgates and allow our prayers to be unhindered and transcend this world to the throne room of God.

2. "We forgive!" is our cry. Because of these two words, our prayers come into agreement and alignment with the prayers that our Beloved Bridegroom and Great Intercessor is already making on our behalf. The hallowing of His name and the shouts of triumph echo forth as all of heaven hears and awaits the instruction of the Great Judge...our Abba Daddy. He hears the cries of His Son as He represents us in the courtroom of Heaven. The pleas and arguments come forth; the verdict goes out and angels are dispatched to do His bidding. Thank You for planting the initiative of forgiveness in us.

3. Even when others don't follow this path, we do. We do not allow ourselves the right to have rights. We have released them to You. We will burn with the passion to forgive whenever, whoever, wherever, and for whatever the need may demand. Our eyes are upon You, our Lord and King. We have taken them off **our** hurts...**our** pains...**our** rights...**our** ways...**our** plans...**our** agendas...**our** options. We will not tire of seeking Your strength to do this. We declare this loudly as a

constant reminder that we have given up the options to dwell on ourselves. Our eyes are on You alone.

4. When we feel we can't go on, we stop. Then we seek Your presence and Your peace. This gives us the strength and courage we need. We pray that we will never allow thoughts to become so overwhelming that we give in to them and allow them to control us. We choose to have only one Master—YOU, **El Shaddai** (Lord God Almighty), **El Elyon** (The Most High God), **Adonai** (Lord, Master), **Yahweh** (Lord, Jehovah), **Jehovah Nissi** (The Lord My Banner), **Jehovah-Raah** (The Lord My Shepherd), **Jehovah Rapha** (The Lord That Heals), **Jehovah Shammah** (The Lord Is There), **Jehovah Tsidkenu** (The Lord Our Righteousness), **Jehovah Mekoddishkem** (The Lord Who Sanctifies You), **El Olam** (The Everlasting God), **Elohim** (God), **Qanna** (Jealous), **Jehovah Jireh** (The Lord Will Provide), **Jehovah Shalom** (The Lord Is Peace), and **Jehovah Sabaoth** (The Lord of Hosts).

5. You are the One who takes our breath away. With every beat of our heart, we trust You to help us align ourselves with You. We want to be all that You want us to be. The path of forgiveness leads and guides us. With heartfelt, real-life forgiveness active in us, we become the person God created us to be. We want to walk through life reaching our full potential. "Release"—that is our plea. We hear You clearly…"Forgive all and become unoffendable!"

6. "Yes," we cry; "Yes," to You. That is our goal. We can do this because You live inside of us. Allow Your spirit to teach us and guide us in the way we should go (Ps. 32:8 paraphrased) …then and only then will we not depart from it. Even though the enemy has other plans and tries to get us off-track, we say, "No!" It is a violent and vehement NO—one that is decisive and causes us to do what is right. It forces a heavenly alignment to take place. Our hearts say, "Yes," but we still cry, "Help us Lord! Help! We choose to forgive and to be unoffendable, so that our prayers reach heaven" (Matt. 18:35 paraphrased). In the name of Jesus, Amen!

Six
Healing

Dedicated to Russell Long

"He sent his word, and healed them, and delivered them from their destructions" (Psalms 107:20 KJV).

"Surely he took up our infirmities and carried our sorrows, yet we considered him stricken by God, smitten by him, and afflicted. But he was pierced for our transgressions, he was crushed for our iniquities; the punishment that brought us peace was upon him, and by his wounds we are healed (Isaiah 53:4-5 NIV).

"Surely he hath borne our griefs, and carried our sorrows: yet we did esteem him stricken, smitten of God, and afflicted. But he was wounded for our transgressions, he was bruised for our iniquities: the chastisement of our peace was upon him; and with his stripes we are healed" (Isaiah 53:4-5 KJV).

1. From the depths of our being to the highest of heights, we will praise You. We will sing out praise to You and for You, our God and King. How majestic are Your ways, O Lord. How incredible are Your thoughts toward us. We thank You in the midst of our situations that You are Jehovah Rapha, the Lord that heals.

2. Where can we go from You? If we go to the Heavens, You are there. If we flee to the depths, You are there" (Ps. 139:8 paraphrased). You are a living God. You heal us and see us through every difficult situation. You are the One who lays the path out before us and says, *"Whether you turn to the right or to the left, your ears will hear a voice behind you, saying, 'This is the way; walk in it'"* (Isa. 30:21 NIV).

3. We keep to Your path because we understand Your ways through Your word. You want to heal us; You want to deliver us from our own destructive ways and tendencies. Your path will lead us there. Your path took You to the cross to bear our iniquities and sorrow. The stripes You bore were given for us to gain access to all that You did

for us on the cross. Our debt is paid in full. Thank you for these three small words, *"It is finished!"* (John 19:30 NIV).

4. We appropriate this complete work today—knowing that it is for us. We are healed. You made our innermost being, and all our days were numbered by You beforehand (Ps. 139: 16 paraphrased). You understand everything about us and love us just as we are. You gaze upon us and know that we are fearfully and wonderfully made (Ps. 139:14 paraphrased). We rejoice in this fact even when things in our body don't cooperate. We never give up on You.

5. In the midst of all this, we walk from facts (what the doctors and our bodies are reporting) into the truth—*by His stripes we are healed* (Is. 53:5 paraphrased). *He sent His word to heal us* (Ps. 107:20 paraphrased). We look with spiritual eyes as best as we are able. We command our bodies to align with all that is true, right, and good. We don't lie; yet, we trust the One who died on the cross for us. It is the finished work in which we place our hope, belief, and trust.

6. Your word says, and we believe it, *"Surely he hath borne our griefs, and carried our sorrows: yet we did esteem him stricken, smitten of God, and afflicted. But he was wounded for our transgressions, he was bruised for our iniquities: the chastisement of our peace was upon him; and with his stripes we are healed"* (Isa. 53:4-5 KJV).

7. What could be better than Your word applied to our situations? Our minds perceive it, but how do we receive it in actuality? It is such a mystery. It is the mystery of the cross and Your Kingdom…an understanding that You did a complete work. We cry out and pray to know how to receive all that You did for us. So, daily we plead with our Savior, "Teach us how to pray; teach us how to receive!" You are the God who heals us. You are God, and in You is <u>no lack</u>.

8. This imperfect vessel cries out to walk in this, fulfilling that which You fulfilled at the cross. "Please help us!" is our cry. "We are unable to ascertain this unless You help us." Then peace comes, and we know You have heard our supplication. *"Thy will be done on earth as it is in Heaven"* (Matt. 6:10 KJV). Even amid this trial, we choose not to stress; instead we receive Your peace, which *passes all understanding (Phil, 4:7 paraphrased).* We will seek more of You daily with every breath and all our being! In the name of Jesus, Amen.

Seven
Let's Not Grow Weary

Dedicated to Karen Fraley Coey and Becky Sparks Hitchens

"And let us not be weary in well doing: for in due season we shall reap, if we faint not" (Gal. 6:9 KJV).

"Anyone, then, who knows the good he ought to do and doesn't do it, sins" (James 4:17 NIV).

1. Speak, declare, shout, and sing to all who have ears to hear, **"We serve a holy God."** The Lord tells us to be holy for He is holy! (1Pt. 1:16 paraphrased). Therefore, we take this approach to all things to the best of our ability. We stand ready to decree Your word and wait for it to perform all that You intend for the Word to perform. We do not…we cannot…we will not…grow "weary in well doing" (Gal. 6:9 KJV).

2. Our eyes are upon You, Most High God and King. Therefore, we take the Word of God seriously. We don't want to sin. We confess ours sins when we do. We can't escape this one thing…if we know what we're supposed to be doing (the Bible teaches us this) and yet we do otherwise, then we have sinned (James 4:17 paraphrased). Lord, this is so easy to understand, but so difficult to do.

3. Everywhere we look, we see the opposite taking place. Therefore, our cry to You is for HELP! Your word tells us to be quick to listen (James 1:19 paraphrased). How do we do this? Habits are set up in our lives and take us to a place of valuing our thoughts and ways rather than Your truth. We repent, seek Your face, and turn from our ways to Yours.

4. Help us be slow to speak so that our words don't become lofty and we suffer the same fate as Job's friends. Allow the words that come forth to be like the *pen of a ready writer.* (Ps. 45:1 paraphrased) *…apples of sliver in settings of gold* (Pr. 25:11 NIV) …not mere words that accomplish nothing but oppress the listener and fall to the ground. They are of no value. Allow our words to be what's on God's heart

and in tune with the symphony of heaven: on key, pleasing and full of melodious sounds that come together like a symphony to the hearers.

5. The ways of the world can cause our blood to boil with anger and frustration. Yet, Your word warns us: *be slow to become angry* (James 1:19 paraphrased). We say, "Yes," and try to heed that; but, we hear of the atrocities against the unborn and the defamation against our Lord and Savior. We can barely take it. So, we ask You to teach us the difference between righteous anger and anger that erupts from our souls. Our souls produce that which pleases the flesh and can be demonic in its origin—producing sinful responses; yet, righteous anger is in sync with heaven and reverberates Biblical wisdom from God, our Creator. Our goal is to bring delight to You...help us be those who go above and beyond to please You, King Jesus.

6. Holy Spirit, we need Your guidance and grace to traverse this. We give You permission to engage our spirit-man at all times. We don't want to be fleshly driven, giving into the anger that loves to burn and spew forth words that do not bring pleasure to heaven and its host. Holy Spirit, help us and cause our spirit to connect to You instead of our fleshly ways and nature.

7. Everywhere we look people defame the name of God, using it with such ignorance, distaste and ingratitude. We cry out, "Help us do the opposite, being those who brings glory to Your name, rightly dividing the word of God (2 Tim. 2:15 paraphrased) and expressing truth to a lost and dying people." May our words be heavenly inspired—supernatural in character, producing swift results...Let the consequence of our words be eternal in disposition—making a difference on this earth and forever. It's all about YOU! May we truly live Your Word and do what is right. May we be doers of Your Word so that we walk, talk, and act uprightly...in a way that pleases You. Help us have words that are sweet going out to the hearer. Help, Abba Daddy. This is our cry; this is our plea, and we ask it in the mighty, magnificent name of Jesus. Amen.

Eight
You can Run; but You Can't Hide…

Dedicated to Emily Fauk, Betty Kozlowski, Jacqueline Teagle, Nancy Hughes and Paul Schneider

"But if I drive out demons by the Spirit of God, then the kingdom of God has come upon you" (Matt. 12:28 NIV).

"But if I drive out demons by the finger of God, then the kingdom of God has come to you" (Luke 11:20 NIV).

1. We stand amazed in Your presence, Lord! We stand amazed that You would ever consider using us to advance Your Kingdom. Yet, in this one name…JESUS (of Nazareth) …demons tremble and flee; sickness is healed; people are saved! The Kingdom of God advances and is released. So, we choose today to scream it out (JESUS), shout it from the rooftops (JESUS), declare it at the top of our lungs (JESUS). Your name is precious and powerful…JESUS!

2. We can feel it. The earth responds. There is trembling, shaking, shifting, and stirring. There is gasping, breathing, begging, and birthing. This happens every time Your name is whispered, spelled, spoken, or shouted. All of it produces Your good will and pleasure (Phil. 2:13 paraphrased). Yeah! We get to be a part of it. You choose us whether we're having a good day or bad—whether we're happy or sad. We see it and shout it out! "It's all about You every day, all the time, and in every way!" What an awesome God we serve!

3. This is what we hear and come into agreement with. *"On your mark, get set, go!"* That's how we start each day. Anticipation for what lies ahead summons us, and we say "Yes!" We know that wherever we go, our footsteps cause realms to stir and shift. We take ground for God because You live in us. Every place we go is a chance to advance the Kingdom. We pray, "Give us eyes to see and ears to hear. Help us make the most of every opportunity—doing and praying what is on the Father's heart."

4. We step out, laying hands on the sick, praying for the lost, and casting out demons. Freely we have received, so freely we give (Matt. 10:8 paraphrased). Lord, we stand ready—like a good soldier. We want to hear You as never before and do specifically what You're saying. Obedience is the key. Help us not strike out, but to hit the target. Help us to know when to speak and when to remain silent.

5. Teach us how to pray what's on Your heart, not ours. Help us to understand the supernatural and how to operate within the heavenly guidelines and parameters. We long to drive out demons and *know that we know* that the Kingdom of God has advanced. We want to pray the most effective way...getting to the answer by going the quickest route.

6. Evil entities lurk, waiting and hiding. They know we're coming for them. They may run and hide, but, we operate in the gifts of the spirit—the weapons of our warfare. Our tool belts are full and ready for use at a moment's notice. It could be in church, on the phone, in a prayer meeting, at a restaurant or possibly while shopping. We thank You, Lord, that You have trained our hands and fingers for battle (Ps. 144:1 paraphrased) and we are able warriors. You have taught us how to make surgical strikes, so we cry out and You answer...The results: ***another demon bites the dust!***

7. Daily You hear our pleas and answer our prayers. So we cry out, "Use us to advance Your Kingdom, to set the captives free." We want to feel the presence of our King and God! How lovely You are! Surely You have chosen us. We see it happening continually...demons are driven out by the spirit of God that lives within us. Selah! I pause to consider...why would the God of the Universe ever consider using us, mere mortals? It is unbelievable...incredible...unfathomable. We stand in awe and give thanks. It's all we've ever wanted, and Your answer is "YES!" What more can we say, except thank You for allowing us to participate with You in these supernatural endeavors, in the mighty name of Jesus! Amen.

Nine
Opening Doors that no Man Can Shut

Dedicated to Pete II and Erika Mullins, and David and Catherine Robbins

"These things says he who is holy, he who is true, he who has the key of David, opening the door so that it may be shut by no one, and shutting it so that it may be open to no one" (Rev. 3:7 BBE).

1. Father, we come today, holding a prayer key—the key of David. We don't want anything but Your will to be done in our lives and those we love. Yet, sometimes *Your will* evades us. We don't know what to pray. We don't know what to say or ask for. We don't have the solution.

2. Yielding all to You, we simply pray, "Would You open Your door of destiny for _____ (name your church), our families, and us? (Name any situation or specific door that needs to be opened at this time.) Our plea to heaven resounds. Would You close every door that is not Your plan? Would it be such that no man could open it once You've closed it; and no man can close it once You've opened it?" (Rev. 3:7 paraphrased). In other words, let it be only Your will coming forth. We are no longer satisfied with Your permissive will. We must walk in the perfect will of God.

3. Our flesh wants to interfere in this process. It is weak. Yet, we know that Your strength in our lives is what we need. Therefore, we set our faces like flint, trusting You in the midst of our weaknesses and every circumstance. We choose to believe You for the outcomes. Help us to seek You in all things, realizing, *"Your grace **IS** sufficient!"* (2 Cor. 12:9 paraphrased).

4. We shout for all to hear, "We serve God!"—the One who is **all** seeing, **all** knowing, **all** powerful, and **ever** present. He alone gives us keys that bring heaven to earth…*His will, not ours*…the sufficiency of all that is needed at the exact right time for every circumstance.

5. We do our best to back off and remove our hands from the situation. *(HELP US DO THIS, LORD!)* We Cast this upon the Lord, and our prayers release the King of Kings and Lord of Lords. You are arranging things on our behalf, doing only what You see the Father doing; saying only what is right and glorious—what the Father is saying (John 5:19 paraphrased).

6. Our pleas reach heaven, opening and closing doors—heaven comes to earth. Our faith arises as we look into the eyes of our Beloved. Your perfect will, not ours... Your ways, not some fleshly desire. How magnificent this is! We are completely abandoned to the One who bought our salvation. We realize this is for our good, but mostly for Your glory.

7. Ultimately, we yield ourselves and every situation to You...this makes all the difference. Once again, we see that Your ways are higher than ours. You respond to the sound of our voices, causing each situation to bow and align with heaven as we pray, releasing the key of David. We watch in delight as God hooks eternity into the here and now. Come, Holy Spirit! Help us to know when to pray this. Guide us into all truth. Thank You for this tool...this key...this prayer, in Jesus' name, Amen.

Ten
Rejoice in the Lord Always

Dedicated to Kathy Peters and my sacred sisters—Wanda Mardis, Diane Calsbeek, Darlene Lovett, and Stacey Smith

"Rejoice in the Lord always. I will say it again: Rejoice!" (Phil. 4:4 NIV).

1. Today is a day of rejoicing! That is our choice. We choose to rejoice in You our Lord and King...in all You are... in all You've done...We will not stop rejoicing until it reaches heaven and we see a smile on Your face. All You've accomplished has made us glad. We refrain from dwelling on other things—incomplete and undone work lying before us. Our thoughts are on You and You alone.

2. We have seen You do great and mighty things. This is cause for celebration. We have seen You come forth as the One Who Battles and Wins Victories on our behalf. We have seen You as the One Who Promises and Delivers...the One Who is Silent, saying, "Not now, My children." Yet, this is for our good, but ultimately for Your glory.

3. Lord, we adore You with all that we are today. We enthrone You in our hearts once again. We give You permission to release the fresh oil for today. We are so full of thanksgiving that our hearts explode and pour forth pure love for You, the Lover of our souls. Nobody can take this away from us; our spiritual roots go down deep and wide. False winds of doctrine cannot dissuade us. No...the fire of God burns bright within us. You see this and remain glad.

4. Our delight is in You. This transforms every part of us, bringing a divine connection. All that are around us wonder what it is. It's not *what but WHO*...the Bridegroom. That's why we continue to make ourselves ready (Rev. 19:7 paraphrased), rejoicing day and night in YOU! Our lamps are full of oil; the Holy Spirit is alive and active in us. We sense Your presence. Our spirits leap with joy.

5. Thanks for all that You do in and through us. We know that the Kingdom of God advances. It is here—within and around us. When we

step out, ground is taken for the Kingdom. The enemy retreats as we rejoice. How cool is that? Thank You, Jesus, for marvelous times of rejoicing in You and through You, bringing us one step closer to destiny fulfilled and the promise of our salvation being realized. What a time of rejoicing, in the mighty name of Jesus, amen and amen!

Eleven
Destiny is the Goal

Dedicated to Sherrelle Giles, Jonathan and Mary Beth Mullins

"Yet I still belong to you; you hold my right hand. You guide me with your counsel, leading me to a glorious destiny. Whom have I in heaven but you? I desire you more than anything on earth" (Ps. 73:23-25 NLT).

1. Lord, how we praise and adore You. Allow our voices to be clear and sustained, like that of a youth—even into our latter years. Allow praise, glory, adoration, worship, teaching, and preaching come forth and ring out for all to hear. Don't allow the trailing of our voices and vocal weariness ever to be something that stops what You have placed in us to do.

2. We say, "Voice, come forth in strength, power, and might" that all may hear and know that we serve the One True God, and that He has given us something to preach, pray, and sing about! We worship You, Almighty God; there is NONE like You!

3. Our hearts rejoice in this thought! So, we declare it for all to hear and know. We will not be silenced when it comes to the King of Kings and Lord of Lords! You alone are worthy...You alone are worthy...You alone are worthy! We command even our vocal cords to align with the purposes and plans of the Kingdom of God. Let's never grow weary in well doing.

4. Coughing must cease. Laryngitis must go. Allergies and asthma must desist. Sore throat, tiredness, vocal pain, cancer and/or nodules of any type must bow to the name of Jesus and the finished work of the cross. We command *Destiny Stealer* to get off our vocal cords, out of our throats, and away from us. We will not give into demonic forces, nor will we sit idly by while *it* comes to rob, destroy, kill, or steal from us or any of God's children who are working out their salvation and God-ordained destiny. This is not optional.

5. We sit up, take notice, and fight for that which Jesus fought for us and obtained. It happened in an instant when He said, "It is finished" (John

19:30 NIV). We come into agreement with this and receive what this means in Heaven while we're still on the earth. Our plea is simple… "Let not one jot or tittle go unfinished that God had planned for us before the creation of the world (Eph. 1:4 paraphrased). Let every breath within us breathe for one purpose and one purpose alone: may Your will be done on earth through us as it is in Heaven (Matt. 6:10 paraphrased)—nothing more…nothing less…Your will and Your will alone."

6. Our cry today is that "Destiny" would be achieved in our lives and that every hindrance would be thwarted right now…now and forever. Strength is one of the virtues we put on as a mantle. It allows us to be sustained in youth, middle age, or as a senior citizen. Let the beauty of Your holiness continue to flow through us as we walk with integrity and uprightness—clothed in You. This is our mantle of distinction.

7. We live fearlessly for You. This comes forth loud and clear. Those who know us marvel at what You're doing and saying through us as vessels set apart to You. We hear and believe, *"The sky's the limit."* We respond with vigor, filled with anticipation, yet laced with humility as we take Your hand and call out, "Come on Jesus! Let's do this thing called Destiny together." You echo back my name with a holy, "Yes!"

8. As we kneel before You in adoration, we can hardly believe that You want to use us, and the only goal You have is that we fulfill what You created us to do. It's like a hand-in-glove…destiny. That's our goal and our prayer, in the mighty name of Jesus. Destiny, arise and come forth! Amen.

Twelve
Sowing and Reaping

Dedicated to Donna Smith

"Do not be deceived: God cannot be mocked. A man reaps what he sows. The one who sows to please his sinful nature, from that nature will reap destruction; the one who sows to please the Spirit, from the Spirit will reap eternal life. Let us not become weary in doing good, for at the proper time we will reap a harvest if we do not give up. Therefore, as we have opportunity, let us do good to all people, especially to those who belong to the family of believers" (Gal. 6:7-10 NIV).

1. Heavenly Father, Your ways are so much higher than ours; Your thoughts above what we can think or imagine (Is. 55:8 paraphrased). But, this one thing we do, we put behind us all that is not YOU and press forward to the calling that You have for us. We press to obtain the fullness of You (Phil. 3:13-14 paraphrased). Therefore, we rid ourselves of the former things…the old ways, to take up what is on Your heart for today.

2. We can only imagine what You have in store for us when we're about what pleases the Father. Our imaginations run wild thinking of ways to please Abba Daddy. Knowing that Your word commands, "Do not be deceived," (Gal. 6:7 NIV) that is a key for all who have ears to hear. We look around and see so many that fail to obey and then reap a whirlwind of destruction. Don't let that be us, Lord. We don't want anything we do to mock or displease You. We do not delight in the resulting devastation that is produced.

3. We repent of sowing to *ourselves*—that ugly, sinful nature that demands its way and produces a self-fulfilling prophecy of heartache and pain that results in ruin to our loved ones and us. Our hearts are set on doing right; but, when we least expect it, deception seizes us. It engulfs, entraps, and ensnares us. It produces the vilest results that we do not want. Our cry to this lack of self-discipline and self-control is, "NO!" We are no longer availing ourselves to the spirits behind this lukewarm attitude and wickedness.

4. Instead, we yield our members to righteousness leading to holiness—sowing to please the Holy Spirit of Almighty God, our Comforter and Teacher. You are the only One whom we desire to please. You are the One who whispers, "Come up higher," and we respond with a wholehearted, "Yes!" We combine this with action. Words without deeds are empty and fall to the ground. That is not who we are!

5. We love on You, Jesus, with bold and speedy obedience, doing good to all people, knowing that we are laying up for ourselves Heavenly treasure that will not rust or fade. Rather, we produce what You intend; we do not become weary in well doing or get easily sidetracked. Our hearts break for those who *talk the talk,* but do not *walk the walk—unfaithful to the core—*yet wanting to do right.

6. Hearts are hardened, fraught with the potholes of life brought about by deception—not understanding that there is a Biblical law in place called *sowing and reaping.* How can a loving God allow this? Your word says plainly, *"God cannot be mocked"* (Gal. 6:7 NIV). (That means You **will not** be…it is a supernatural impossibility!) Our plea is that we have the grace to continually walk in the Holy Spirit *dunamis* power living in us to do what is right and pleasing to You. "Help us not be deceived, O Lord!" This cry goes out for our families, churches, and friends also.

7. Help us not give up due to past failures. *Your mercies are new every morning* (Lam. 3:23 paraphrased). We receive it for today. We receive it for every moment of temptation. We open our eyes and walk in wisdom, sowing to the Spirit and reaping the benefits. Allow us to recognize and activate Your will for us at all times. We know it will lead to a rich harvest of well doing. This spills over to the family of believers, and is one of the ways we walk in God's plan for our lives. Help us to be known as those who are about the Father's business, "*doing good,*" especially to the body of Christ.

8. Thank You, Lord, for spelling it out clearly so that we can understand Your ways. We thank You *for making a way when there seems to be no way* and helping us *walk the walk* You have for us. We praise You for this in the mighty and fabulous name of Jesus! Amen.

Thirteen
Delight Yourself in the Lord

Dedicated to Ashley Schultz and Cheryl Hanson

Trust in the LORD and do good; dwell in the land and enjoy safe pasture. Delight yourself in the LORD and he will give you the desires of your heart. Commit your way to the LORD; trust in him and he will do this: He will make your righteousness shine like the dawn, the justice of your cause like the noonday sun. Be still before the LORD and wait patiently for him (Ps. 37:3-7 NIV).

1. Abba, Daddy…We stop and pause at this one thought…this one insight, *"Delight yourself in the Lord"* (Ps. 37:4 NIV). Do we even have the slightest idea of how to do this? Our cry today is, "Teach us to delight ourselves in You." Show us how to bring You *great enjoyment and pleasure*—the dictionary definition of *delight*.

2. Our hearts are fully devoted to this one thing today: bringing pleasure to You, our King. We begin our days basking in the sunlight of that thought. It warms our insides and our spirit-man comes alive. Even our heartbeat speeds up as we come into agreement with this scripture. We prayerfully question the One who can save to the uttermost, "What is required of us, and how do we do it?" If we think too long, we may become overwhelmed. What do we possess that we can present a king, especially the King of Kings?

3. Your word cajoles us: *"delight yourself in the Lord."* Then, we will *receive the desires of our heart* (Ps. 37:4 paraphrased). Is that the goal? At first-glance it appears so. These heart-desires have been put there by You anyway. Yet, that is *so not* **it**, even though it transpires. First and foremost, it is Your breath in us, Your loving kindness flowing through us, and Your mercy toward us, which we receive as we delight in You. It's Your presence. It's the encounter of the living-ness of the living God. It is a touch from Heaven reaching into our being and the finger of God bringing exactly what is needful—YOU. This is what we want; this is our prayer; this is the essence of delighting in You. Other things come forth, but they are only secondary to an encounter with the King of Glory.

4. Of course, we long to obtain the desires of our heart that You have placed within us. But there is *more,* and we want the ***more***. This comes because we choose freely to accept the discipline of delighting in the *Alpha and Omega, the First and the Last, the Beginning and the End* (Rev. 22:13 NIV*), who is, and was and who is to come…* (Rev. 1:8 NIV). We do this with help from the Holy Spirit, even when we don't feel like it. We decree what is <u>not so</u>, so that in God's timing <u>it will be so</u>! That's what we're releasing in faith today.

5. As we linger in prayer, You answer. It is, "Yes." We have asked to be taught and You have done it as we've pleaded, sought, and waited. Our minds cannot comprehend this; yet, our spirit leaps with joy, drinking in Your presence, thirsting for more of You. Our spirit connects with Your spirit and we receive a touch from the Lord. We want more. We want to be clothed with this tangible presence all the time. "Help us," we cry out.

6. And so You do. But, it begins with us. We must delight in You. Daily, we cry out for accelerated ability to delight in You in greater measures. Release this in exponential ways! The desires of our heart change as we obey this scripture. As we go forward, we ask less and less for the carnal things of this world. We appreciate the blessings that pour forth from a life well-lived *for* You and *by* You and *through* You. But more than that, we long and pant for the pure pleasure of Your presence which You bring as we delight in You.

7. We cry out for the tangible and the supernatural presence of Almighty God. Hear us as we call. Your answer is so simple…"Take delight in me," You say, "And surely I will give you the desires of your heart (Ps. 37:4 paraphrased). Don't be surprised if these desires change along life's journey." We are fascinated by this and continue our plea for help. We can't thank You enough, but try to as we experience this newfound joy, freedom, and tangible presence that comes. We are forever thankful to our Abba Daddy, in the mighty name of Jesus. Amen.

Fourteen
His Grace is Sufficient

Dedicated to Cathy Goddard, Julie Hunt, and Marilyn and Ray Boyle, my mother and late step-father

"To keep me from becoming conceited because of these surpassingly great revelations, there was given me a thorn in my flesh, a messenger of Satan, to torment me. Three times I pleaded with the Lord to take it away from me. But he said to me, "My grace is sufficient for you, for my power is made perfect in weakness" (2 Cor. 12:7-9 NIV).

1. We cry out to You, Abba Father, Daddy, in the one and only mighty magnificent name, Jesus…knowing, declaring, and pleading Your word over our situations. The day appears bleak and uninviting. The enemies of our souls stand ready to pounce if we display the slightest weakness. They do not realize that our weakness is only an opportunity for the manifest strength of God to be released (1Cor. 12:9 paraphrased).

2. Releasing demonic plans at just the right moment and creating a whirlwind of absolute destruction, their objective is to distract us and bring unequivocal defeat. The target: annihilation of all that we were created for and all we've lived toward achieving—God's DESTINY. The demonic end game: to not finish the race God has set before us.

3. It is the perfect storm, sent to separate us from the Lord—my beloved Bridegroom, neutralizing all that His blood bought. Yet, we stand unafraid, knowing that the *testing of our faith produces perseverance* (James 1:3 paraphrased). We will finish this race! Praying, we quote the word and stand on it, *"Your grace IS sufficient!"* (2 Cor. 12:9 paraphrased). We shout it from the housetops for all to hear, "We will not back down; we will not give in; we will not relinquish ground!" We bellow it to all the attackers, seen and unseen, **"Do you hear me?"**

4. Our Abba Daddy does. Our Bridegroom does. The Holy Spirit does. All three coordinate their efforts. Jesus, at the right hand of the Father, is making intercession for us. He says and does only what God the Father is saying and doing. The Holy Spirit honors the rest of the

Godhead by illuminating God's plans through us, mere mortals. The living-ness of God on the earth flows to us, in us and through us. We are not defeated! We are more than conquerors. We know it. We believe it. We shout it. We decree it. We don't stand in God's way. Our body, soul, and spirit come into agreement with the blueprints of Heaven.

5. We are not defeated! We are alive with Your presence. The forces of darkness may try to destroy us, but our prayers are like a wall that surrounds us. God protects us with all the might of heaven. Is it in the form of light? Is it the very essence of His presence...His anointing...His glory? Is it the angelic host sent to minister to those who will inherit salvation? Is it warring angels? Is it all of this or a combination? We don't know.

6. When we ask, You come. When we seek, You are found (Matt. 7:7-8 paraphrased). God stands and knocks. We open. You come in; we sup together (Rev. 3:20 paraphrased). How can that be? Our cry is, "Help." You say, "Yes!" Your word is performed. It is You, not us. Your presence comes. It's a mystery our minds cannot comprehend. It is the sufficiency of Your grace manifest in manifold ways, full of wisdom from on high, released to the here and now... Your word performed in the land of the living.

7. Yes, we're walking-talking-breathing examples. *Your grace is sufficient for us . . . Your grace is sufficient for us . . . Your grace is sufficient for us . . .* (2 Cor. 12:9 paraphrased). That is the truth, and we thank You for all You've done in Jesus' mighty name. Amen.

Fifteen
God is for Us

Dedicated to Patrick and Sipra Singh

"What shall we then say to these things? If God be for us, who can be against us? He that spared not his own Son, but delivered him up for us all, how shall he not with him also freely give us all things?" (Rom. 8:31-32 KJV).

1. We read it, declare it and come into agreement with Romans 8:31-32 **now**. If God be for us *(He is!)*, who can be against us? The enemy tries in many ways, setting traps to ensnare us; the world beckons us to come hither; yet in reality, we are the only ones who can open the door to sin and allow it in. Thank You, Lord, that nothing can be against us…but us.

2. *Our spirits are willing, but our flesh is weak* (Mark 14:38 paraphrased). Therefore, we cry out for what we see within us and those around us. We know You love Your Church and bride. So today, we release over ourselves, our families, (name your church) _____, and all Christian believers everywhere, the ability to comprehend and grasp that God is truly in love with His Church. He wants all to be included.

3. Let it be an individual and corporate revelation. Start with us! Let it go forth from the pages of scripture to our minds, written on our hearts. Allow this understanding to penetrate deeply. May it produce a life of action dedicated to King Jesus. Our spirit-man connects with heaven and the response is, "Yes!"

4. We want all that You have for us. We want to stand amid every situation—even in the fray of the battle—knowing that the God of the universe is for us, fighting our battles, tending to our wounds, whispering words of love, and anointing us with the oil of gladness. It is not beyond receiving; but it is too much for our minds to comprehend. Wrapped in the holiness of His arms, we shout again, "Yes, we want You and all that You have for us!"

5. We want to delight in the pleasure of knowing You and sensing the slightest move You make. You are God; there is none that compares with You! Help us to grasp *how wide and long and high and deep is the love of Christ* (Eph. 3:18 NIV) for us! Our prayer is that somehow we will be able to worship and adore You every moment with all that we are.

6. Please receive this offering. With all our might, we struggle to give it as freely as You gave Your Son, and as freely as You laid down Your life for us. We want our actions to match our words. Even so, You understand the frailty of our souls. When we are weak, You are strong (2 Cor. 12:9 paraphrased). When we sabotage our lives with sin, You stand ready to forgive. As soon as we repent, You don't remember our sin any longer. With just one glance we are forgiven...restored totally to wholeness, as if we'd never sinned. How can this be?

7. Over and over we long for more of You. We want to know You. We want to feel Your breath upon us and Your fire within us. This is our prayer. Let our lives exist for You; let all that know us see YOU. Allow our lives to be a living epistle that draws others to You and brings them into this same love relationship.

8. How we love You and long to love You more and more. We meditate on You. Our minds race to receive that You are for us all the time (Rom. 8:31 paraphrased) in every circumstance; no demon power from hell can stop that fact! We don't feel worthy to be the recipient of love this amazing; yet it is part of the everlasting covenant that You made with Your blood. Thank You does not seem to be enough. So, we say a simple three-letter word over and over, louder and louder, to communicate to the King of Glory a life-attitude for which there are not adequate human words to express: "Yes...Yes...YES!" Please accept this yes, in the name of Jesus we pray, Amen!

Sixteen
The Prayer of the Bride to the Bridegroom

Dedicated to Amanda and Russell Long, Gary and Shelly Davis, Paul Schneider, Julie Chambliss, and all who long for revival and kingdom transformation.

"Hallelujah! For our Lord God Almighty reigns. Let us rejoice and be glad and give him glory! For the wedding of the Lamb has come, and his bride has made herself ready. Fine linen, bright and clean, was given her to wear" (Fine linen stands for the righteous acts of the saints.) (Rev. 19:6-8).

1. Today we pray a love song to the One we adore…we come as the bride, arrayed in white…who has been and is making herself ready. *You are our beloved and we are Yours. We* linger on that one sentence. *You are ours and we are Yours* (Song of Sol. 6:3 paraphrased). What does that mean amid a dying and perverse generation? Can that one declaration change things and make a difference? We say, "Yes."

2. We come with a made-up mind, entering this day. We will not be persuaded by what we see or hear. We will allow You, the champion of our souls, to rule and reign. We will not give in, go back or cease the momentum of living for the King of Kings. We have chosen You, and You have chosen us. In that moment of time, we were changed forever. Now we live a life for You and You alone.

3. You have preeminence in our thoughts and deeds, in words and actions. We declare it to the north, south, east, and west. We live for You. Every power and principality must eventually bow to You, **so why not now**? Our goal is to see it happen wherever we are and wherever we go. The enemy understands we belong to You and You alone. So, we begin the day with prayer; we enter Your courts with thanksgiving. We come into Your gates with praise (Ps. 118:24 paraphrased). Even now, we declare that this is the day You have made. Our choice is this: we will rejoice and be glad in it (Ps. 100:4 paraphrased).

4. Yes, this is taking place because of You. You are our beloved and we are Yours. We go through the day with Your banner of love over us. Even when times are difficult, we touch this banner, and we can sense Your presence. It is real and tangible. It is the love of the Bridegroom to His bride. We breathe, and it's You. Peace is there. Your peace surrounds us, envelopes us, entwines us...That's what we desire. We choose **You** because You first chose us.

5. We call out to our Groom, "Come into every area of our lives." We find joy in You. We find peace in You. We find the manifestation of Your presence. It is in us, near us, and around us. We don't hold back. We corral all our fleshly ways and place them at Your footstool. We take up only that on which You have breathed a holy *"Yes"*.

6. We will not delay, as we are about the Father's business. We are thankful for this love-relationship and friendship we have with Jesus. Therefore, we know what to do and say. It echoes and mirrors heaven. We won't give into temptation to do it our way or the world's way. The enemy tries to ensnare us, but we declare today: "We will not be tricked nor lulled to sleep. We stand ready!"

7. We have set ourselves up for success: reading the word, praying the word, fellowshipping with those who are running hard after the things of God, being in church, and allowing ourselves to be washed with the word. All of this comes together to spell SUCCESS—not in the worldly sense, but in heaven's eyes. We tell our souls, "We will not stop or slow down. We will not give in or give up. We will not allow our flesh to lead." (We declare, decree, and confess this today, in Jesus' name. We command ourselves to align with that declaration!)

8. We <u>will</u> release Heaven to earth; we <u>will</u> listen and obey; we <u>will</u> feed our spirit man, and it <u>will</u> grow up to its full stature that God ordained before the creation of the world for us. Our flesh bows to this and obeys. The training we put ourselves through is because we have seen how the mighty have fallen, and we declare loudly—"**<u>NOT US!</u>** You can't have us. *We're making ourselves ready"* (Rev. 19:7 paraphrased).

9. It is for the marriage of the Lamb. That is our heart's desire and our heart's cry. Hear us! Help us! Join with us! That decree reverberates through the atmosphere. It continues, gathering momentum. Those with the same heart and spiritual DNA come into sync with this

prayer, and a resounding "YES" explodes the air, bringing Heaven to earth and the love of the Bridegroom for His bride. That's the plan and we won't back down until Your kingdom collides with this earthly kingdom and we see it with our eyes in the land of the living...in the mighty name of Jesus! AMEN and AMEN and AMEN!

Seventeen
His Paths are Beyond Tracing Out

Dedicated to Tommie and Elaine Hayes, and Dawn Wells

"Oh, the depth of the riches of the wisdom and knowledge of God! How unsearchable his judgments, and his paths beyond tracing out!" (Romans 11:33 NIV).

1. O, Father, we come into agreement with these words today, searching for that which appears, at first glance, unsearchable—Your judgments. Our prayer is to join You in tracing paths that are untraceable; to prove to ourselves and others that even though God's wisdom is to a depth that is unfathomable, You desire for us to obtain it.

2. We are riveted, yet overwhelmed, by the mere thought that You came to earth for us. You died and rose for us. We stand in awe at what Your death, burial, and resurrection bought. You did it that we could be set free from sin and death. Your atoning sacrifice established the covenant that we freely walk in.

3. We are cocooned in Your covenant and love that was established at the cross, given freely by Jesus, sent by Abba, Daddy—the Father. *Yes, Your ways are beyond tracing out* (Romans 11:33 paraphrased). We can barely comprehend that You, our Lord and Savior, would freely choose to do this for us. Our faith reaches to grasp this truth, but we are unable to adequately do so. Understanding evades us. Submission is before us; we say, "Yes."

4. You're alive, and we fall into the center of Your provisions. We are king's kids and Your ambassador, representing You to all. While we enjoy this closeness, we tap into Your riches filled with wisdom and knowledge. We are close enough to breathe in Your presence, and just one moment brings a lifetime of understanding. It overwhelms us, establishing peace in our thinking—wisdom combined with knowledge brings results.

5. We inhale You and exhale all that is not You. Our decree is simple, "We give all that we are for Your unsearchable judgments" (Romans

11:33 paraphrased). We command our thoughts, ways, appetites, manners, and customs to align with You, releasing pent-up passion and devotion. The kicking and screaming of our carnal ways align with holiness at the mention of Your name.

6. Understanding comes; but it is not immediate. We have an *a-ha moment* as the Holy Spirit, our Comforter and Teacher, guides us to truth. At the same time, we whisper, "Just one glance...one touch...one moment with You—our King!" This shines Your light and establishes our ways.

7. Our prayer and desire is simple—our life devoted to You—set free by Calvary to be all that You called us to be. We speak alignment to ourselves, families, and _____ (name church) to become all that Your design requires. Destiny is our past, present, and future. We step into Your ways, thoughts, paths, and deeds—those that are beyond tracing out, full of the riches of wisdom and knowledge. We do this declaring, "You are worthy to receive all glory, honor, and praise" ...in the mighty name of Jesus. Amen!

Eighteen
The Lord is My Portion

Dedicated to Joseph Tillman and The Ramp, Hamilton, Alabama

"The Lord is my portion," says my soul, "therefore I will hope in him"
(Lam. 3:24 ESV).

1. In the midst of every trial and heartache, we declare to our souls, "The Lord is our portion!" (Therefore we have hope.) We shout to the naysayers, "The Lord is our portion!" (Therefore we have hope.) We decree it to the forces that have set themselves up against us, "The Lord is our portion!" (Therefore we have hope.) This is our just reward, and in this we rest and have peace. Yet, sometimes life is difficult. So please hear our plea for help.

2. Even when things are going smoothly, let our cry be the same, "The Lord is our portion!" Therefore, we **will not**, **cannot**, **do not** fret. We command our emotions to align, and we set our gaze on You, the Author and Finisher of our faith. There is no doubt where our triumph lies—in You and You alone.

3. How magnificent are Your ways toward us. How tremendous are Your thoughts. We can scarcely believe that You are for us and not against us. You have set our feet on solid ground. You have aligned our thoughts. We think on You. We ask for Your help and You say, "Yes!"

4. The King of the Universe—the Most High God displays His beauty for all to see. At times it is seen in the most unlikely place—us. Knowing this gives You pleasure; our request is that You flow through us. Allow others to know You because of what they see in us. Help us to freely give, being about the Father's business. May we realize that it is for one reward—YOU. You are our great reward. You reward us with You—our portion. We breathe, drink, and absorb You into every fiber of our being as we go about our daily business. Yet, we continually give You away. Our portion is supernatural and never runs out.

5. May we not look back or dwell on former things that are unimportant for today. May we never take for granted all that You've done and all we've received. May we allow Your presence to come in such a tangible way that our breath and Yours are in unison; our hearts beat in sync with heaven; our minds are in focus with You—our great reward.

6. What else is there that can compare to the portion we have? What can come close? The answer is easy: no person or anything the world has to offer. So, we stop the comparison. Our search leads only to You. Do not allow us to look for love in all the wrong places, nor allow counterfeit portions to appease us. Our flesh is weak; yet, in our failings and sufferings, we are still running hard after You. We are still obtaining that imperishable reward; we are still receiving the interest of our portion. How can that be? Selah.

7. Even in our weaknesses and as the world condemns us, pouring out penalties for the sins we've committed, You continue to pour and pour into our supernatural bank account. It makes no sense to our minds; it is YOU—our portion—even when we don't deserve it and didn't earn it. Your answer is always the same, "My children, YES, I love you. Yes, I died for you. Yes, I'd do it again. Yes, I am your portion." This truth is difficult to comprehend and even more difficult to receive; therefore, our minds wants to deny it. By faith, we accept it and say, "Thank You!"

8. Since we can't earn it, please help us to be worthy of all that Your death represents! Help us not take Your love and mercy for granted. Help us be the ones who says, "Yes," and mean it—even when it does not go our way. Today, this is our decision: "**We fret not,** because *You are our portion and great reward* (Lam. 3:24 paraphrased). We receive this in the mighty name of Jesus." Amen.

Nineteen
I Press

Dedicated to Kathy Elash and my mentoring group, From Called to Chosen

"Not that I have already obtained all this, or have already been made perfect, but I press on to take hold of that for which Christ Jesus took hold of me. Brothers, I do not consider myself yet to have taken hold of it. But one thing I do: Forgetting what is behind and straining toward what is ahead, I press on toward the goal to win the prize for which God has called me heavenward in Christ Jesus" (Phil 3:12-14 NIV).

1. Heavenly Father, we don't claim to be perfect in any way. Yet, we understand that Your word calls us upward to that higher calling in You. We want to obtain that which appears to be unattainable and out of our reach.

2. So, today we declare and decree over our lives, "We <u>will</u> tap into a heavenly principle…the unknown mystery that can only be described as a **BUT GOD…a suddenly from heaven.**" It is not us; it is all You—the living God within. We will not be lackadaisical or lazy; we will PRESS! We won't allow our flesh to rule. We call forth the spirit-man within and press to take hold of that which Jesus took hold of for us on the cross. We allow the finished work to step into our day, and the covenant Your blood bought to transcend our lives.

3. We refuse to dwell on past mistakes and failures; instead we take hold of that which YOU took hold of for us. We don't understand this mystery; so we set ourselves up for victory by simply saying, "Yes," to You. That allows us to come into agreement with this scripture.

4. We declare, "Old thinking must go." In its place, we allow Your thoughts and presence to encapsulate us. We understand this doesn't happen just because we think it or will it. Instead, day by day…hour by hour…moment by moment, we yield all of us to You—including our thoughts…ways…desires…abilities—even our appetites!

5. We are Yours in every sense that we can be. We know it may be a long and laborious road; yet, we willingly take the route that You have for us. It is not the path of least resistance. It is not the wide road. It is the narrow path. We choose to forget what is behind. We choose to strain for what You have placed ahead of us.

6. We're going for broke, pressing and straining toward the goal—YOU. That is also our prize! We are not satisfied until we see, appropriate, realize, and apportion all that You have for us. While we're on this planet called earth, we continue to strive, to the best of our ability, to serve You, the living God. But, it's for the eternal prize that You have called us to obtain.

7. This is our reality; this is what we desire; this is what we live for. There will be no turning back, no giving up, no yielding to our fleshly ways…we want to live for You, body, soul, and spirit. We want to experience the best us, because we've yielded ourselves to You. We are in the world, not of the world. Our carnal appetites will not rule us, for we know that *greater is He that is in us than he that is in the world* (1John 4:4 paraphrased).

8. Our declaration is that *we will press*; *we will receive the prize*. For we know that our victories lie in You—not anything or anyone else! *You are "the way and the truth, and the life"* (John 14:6 NIV). We are yielded to this—our appetites will not win this fleshly battle, because **today** we've chosen to PRESS, in the mighty name of Jesus! Amen!

Twenty
Cast Your Cares

Dedicated to my First Place 4 Health Class, Newnan, GA

"Cast all your anxiety on him because he cares for you" (1 Peter 5:7 NIV).

"Casting all your care upon him; for he careth for you" (1 Peter 5:7 KJV).

1. Abba, Daddy, we stand amazed at You, casting all our cares upon YOU, for You care for us. We are grateful that as Your children, this is a given—a *done-deal*, so to speak. Therefore, thanksgiving is continually on our lips—the fruit of praise going forth, that You, our King and Lord, are worthy to receive.

2. Our shoulders were not meant to carry all the burdens that life brings our way. When we continually take on additional things that You freely desire to handle, it becomes false burden-bearing on our part, opening the door for the enemy to heap more and more on us until we are crushed under the weight of doing it all ourselves.

3. Today we stop and say, *"No more,"* to every demonic force that has set itself against us. When we've done all we know to do, we stand in faith, knowing that You are dependable in *all things*. We are elated by this and shout praises to You. *"We are the victor, the victim no more!"*

4. Our families and church also benefit from this declaration. This sets them upon Your path, going forward as recipients of the "no greater love" Biblical example. You willingly demonstrated this on the cross for all to see. This evokes praise and worship, prayer and thanksgiving over and over and over again. Our prayers and songs burst forth as a symphony of worship to the only One worthy enough to receive it.

5. We almost feel like an innocent bystander—a pawn, watching what is taking place, and feeling undone by all You do for us. So we fall at Your feet in speechless adoration and awe—words are inadequate. We have a made-up mind that we won't keep this just for us. Our prayer is

that every person we come into contact with will be a recipient of this magnanimous love and grace. Just one glance, and we are undone in Your presence.

6. Thank You that testimony after testimony comes forth from us because we have chosen to obey this scripture and to the best of our ability have carried only that which You required. The treasure of this scripture is seen in the benefits our children, grandchildren, spouse, and extended family receive daily. Because You carried this punishment in Your body on the cross, and we daily release all anxiety to You, miracles are released from heaven and angels are sent to guard our ways.

7. It is a never-ending cycle…We cast our cares upon You…You carry them and release what is needed at the exact perfect time. Everyone who comes in contact with us—friends, family, and associates receive the benefits that come from You carrying the cares we cast upon You. It starts again: we cast our cares upon You… You carry them and release what is needed at the exact perfect time. Everyone who comes in contact with us—friends, family, and associates receive the benefits that come from You carrying the cares we cast upon You. How that brings us solace to our body, soul, and spirit…even our appetites bow in the process. Your ways are so much higher than we can imagine or understand. We give You all praise, glory, and honor due You, in the name of Jesus Christ of Nazareth. Amen and Amen!

Twenty-one
The Lion of the Tribe of Judah Roars

Dedicated to my Coweta Community Church Family

"Listen! Listen to the roar of his voice, to the rumbling that comes from his mouth. He unleashes his lightning beneath the whole heaven and sends it to the ends of the earth. After that comes the sound of his roar; he thunders with his majestic voice. When his voice resounds, he holds nothing back. God's voice thunders in marvelous ways; he does great things beyond our understanding" (Job 37:2-5 NIV).

'"The Lord will roar from on high; He will thunder from his holy dwelling and roar mightily against his land. He will shout like those who tread the grapes, shout against all who live on the earth. The tumult will resound to the ends of earth, for the Lord will bring charges against the nations; He will bring judgment on all mankind and put the wicked to the sword,'" declares the Lord (Jer. 25:30-31 NIV).

The LORD will roar from Zion and thunder from Jerusalem; the earth and the sky will tremble. But the LORD will be a refuge for his people, a stronghold for the people of Israel (Joel 3:16 NIV).

1. Heavenly Father, we hear You say, "I Am roaring from heaven. Do you feel it and hear it? Can you see what I'm doing? I Am releasing my roar; will you participate with me?" What can we say but, "Yes." It may be a weak yes, but it is yes indeed.

2. Allow Your presence to burn within us in such a way that we are overtaken and consumed. Your roar is to get our attention, that of Your bride and remnant. Yet, what does it mean? How do we participate with You? We know it's possible because of the living-ness of Almighty God.

3. You continually show us a new facet of Yourself; yet You change not. We stand in agreement with You, allowing You to overwhelm and overtake our faculties so that we are out of the way and You are what overshadows us—body, soul, and spirit. We come into alignment with

the heavenly roar, capturing hearts of those in need of salvation, repentance from dead works, and sin that so easily entangles.

4. We will not give up nor give in to the ways of the world that are detrimental to all that You stand for and for which You died. We sense You are holding back the floodgates of judgment, standing ready to relent... *if... and... but...*

5. Your roar is for a heartfelt, genuine repentance. Let it be on the hearts and minds of Your people. Let it resound like trumpets that are sounded before a great announcement.

6. *If my people who are called by my name would humble themselves and turn from their wicked ways* (2 Chron.7:14 paraphrased) ...repenting for their words, actions, and deeds...plus that of their nation. We hear You prophetically say, "Would I not willingly hold back the flashes of lightning that heaven thunders, that bring judgment?" (We know You are a good and gracious God.) Yes! You would!

7. Our cry is in unison with heaven. *Your mercies are new every morning* (Lam. 3:23 paraphrased). Show mercy for the sake of Your children and for Your name's sake. We are asking, beseeching, and pleading earnestly. Hear our insistent cry for mercy, peace, and grace. Do not forsake us nor turn Your back. We choose to roar with You. Allow heaven to be released today through Your humble servant. Yes, we roar with You!

8. The despicable practices that have put the angel army on alert have gotten our attention. We are Your soldiers; we release the heavenly roar from the depths of our being today in unison with the Lion of the tribe of Judah. We will not go back; we will not stop; we will not relent until we hear the trumpet sound, the sky split, and see the King of Kings return in glory. To the best of our abilities, we hold nothing back and release this prayer over ourselves, family and church...in the mighty name of Jesus! Amen!

Twenty-two
Have You Not Heard?

Dedicated to Rick Watson

"Do you not know? Have you not heard? The LORD *is the everlasting God, the Creator of the ends of the earth. He will not grow tired or weary, and his understanding no one can fathom. He gives strength to the weary and increases the power of the weak. Even youths grow tired and weary, and young men stumble and fall; but those who hope in the* LORD *will renew their strength. They will soar on wings like eagles; they will run and not grow weary, they will walk and not be faint (Isa. 40:28-31 NIV).*

1. Heavenly Father, we're coming in the mighty name of Jesus, bowing down at Your feet to worship You, enthroning You on our hearts daily. Our utmost and innermost desire is that we would worship You in Spirit and in truth—giving all that we are as an offering to You. Your incredible ways astound us. We know that we know that we know, You have but one goal in mind for us: destiny. This is to advance the Kingdom of God. Your word tells us it is *near us, in us and around us.* (Rom. 10:8 paraphrased*).* We choose to participate with You, listening intently.

2. *"Do you not know? Have you not heard?"* (Is. 40: 21 NIV), echoes within our spirit-man and that brings a hunger and thirst that only You can satisfy. This is the message we want to shout from the housetops to those who have not heard or have forgotten: ***"The*** LORD ***is the everlasting God, the Creator of the ends of the earth"*** (Is. 40:28 NIV). The fullness of this sentence may escape us for a moment; yet, it draws us to You, the lover of our souls. We breathe out. *You don't grow weary* (Is 40:28 paraphrased)—even in the midst of our weariness, trials, and daily routines.

3. You have understanding that we want to comprehend, yet it evades us. So, we trust You for every outcome; we stand in awe of You and how You give us strength when we are weary. In our weakness, You increase our power. You birth through us those things that are on Your

heart that will bring to fruition Your plans that were established *before the creation of the earth.*

4.   We recall this scripture: "I was young and now I am old, yet I have never seen the righteous forsaken or their children begging bread" (Ps. 37:25 NIV). So, we yield ourselves—body, soul, and spirit, knowing that even if *youths grow tired and weary, and young men stumble and fall* (Is. 40:31 paraphrased), we have a secret weapon: YOU! You're faithful to complete and fulfill Your word. It will not…does not…cannot…go out and return without accomplishing the purposes You have sent it forth to do (Is. 55:11 paraphrased). This is our belief and confession. We put our hope in You.

5.   We decree and declare that *our strength is renewed* (Is. 40:31 paraphrased and Job 29:20 NLT paraphrased). It is not the typical rejuvenation that one can easily grasp. Rather, it is of Biblical proportions and of a divine nature because of the covenant promises we walk in. Your word states it; we receive it. *We will soar on wings like eagles. We will run and not grow weary; We will walk and not be faint* (Is. 40:31 paraphrased).

6.   This is not only our hope, but our declaration. We don't merely state it; we attach our faith to these words. We follow the pattern of the eagle. We forsake our natural, carnal, earthly ways and catch the wind of the Spirit. Our soaring can only take place as our faith captures the will of God, and we let go.

7.   Help us today and allow us to ride the waves of the Your Spirit—Your will be done. Help us to stop working in our strength, and instead, yield ourselves to You. Then and only then will we possess this supernatural strength that allows us not to grow weary or faint. Our natural inclination is to want to be in control; but instead we yield that to You. Our prayer and desire is that our strength, thoughts, ways, attitudes, deeds, and ideas would be You, extending through us to all that we encounter.

8.   We yield ourselves daily and receive the fresh oil of anointing. This takes us above our problems and carnal ways. We soar on the atmospheric thermals of Almighty God and proclaim to powers and principalities that we will obey all that the Lord has for us. Our goals and desires are yielded to the point that we can say, "Yes, we do

know! And yes, we have heard!" It is not us but rather You, and all of this is in the mighty name of Jesus. Amen.

Twenty-three
Hearts Fully Committed to YOU

Dedicated to Naphtali and Frank Seamster

"For the eyes of the LORD range throughout the earth to strengthen those whose hearts are fully committed to him" (2 Chron. 16:9 NIV).

"For the eyes of the LORD run to and fro throughout the whole earth, to shew himself strong in the behalf of them whose heart is perfect toward him" (2 Chron. 16:9 KJV).

1. Today, we stop, pause, and meditate on this one thing: *for the eyes of the LORD range throughout the earth to strengthen those whose hearts are fully committed (perfect) to/toward him* (2 Chron. 16:9 paraphrased). Is it even possible for us to claim this as a truth in our lives? Yet, this is our aim. God is our target.

2. We prayerfully release these questions. How can we get more of YOU? More of Your strength? More of Your power? There is but one way…to live a life that is fully devoted to You. We release this thought in prayer today. Help us, Lord. Help us go to the next level of devotion to You—no longer just words spoken from lovesick children, but we want those who look at our lives to read them like an autobiography written to please the King of Kings.

3. So today, we're calling on You to show us what we must do. Teach us how to love You rightly…to love You well…to love You the way that pleases You. Teach us how to serve You in all areas of our lives. When we have been weak and superficial, teach us how to be powerful and profound as a pursuer of God's holiness and righteousness. We want to be the ones that capture the heart and eyes of the Lord.

4. We know that Your eyes are on the sparrow…they're also on us. Yet, we want to capture that one glance of Your eyes that shows that You know You're the *lover of our souls,* and we're sold-out soldiers in the army of God. As You search and indwell us, please, Lord, show Yourself strong on our behalf…mortals whose heart yearns to be perfect toward You. Is that even possible? We don't know; yet, that is

our longing, the very desire of our hearts, and the essence of who we are.

5. We were created to be God-chasers…God-pleasers…those who run hard after You to Shift the Spiritual Atmosphere of our lives, (name your church) _____ and this world. We choose not to grow weary in well-doing. We choose to acknowledge You in all our ways; then You will direct our paths. Thank You for directing it to that timeless place in the spirit where there is no doubt that we are committed and devoted to one thing—YOU!

6. We live, eat, and breathe for God alone. This is our declaration; we shout it for all to hear, "You are *our Beloved and we are Yours.*" (Song of Songs 6:3). To some this may sound crazy; but our quest is to allow this devotion to make a statement. Let this statement be our prayer. Take this prayer and transform us into who You say that we are.

7. We will not back down; we will not stop; we will not allow the enemy of our soul and flesh to win. We will allow God into our lives more fully than ever. You alone are our heart's desire. *Your ways are beyond tracing out* (Rom. 11:33 paraphrased). Your thoughts toward us are as vast as the ocean. Your love is higher than the sky. We have captured that one glance. It has left us undone in Your presence and longing for more of You.

8. Yet we don't stop; we desire another glance…another touch…another insight of knowing. We must have more of YOU. We are addicted to Your presence. One touch leaves us longing for the next. "More" is the cry of our hearts. Hear us. Change us. Help us. Encourage us. Strengthen us. We want to be fully devoted/committed/perfect toward You. This is our prayer, in the name of Jesus, our Savior and Lord. Amen.

Twenty-four
The Breaker Anointing

Dedicated to the women of the Pathway House, Newnan, Georgia

"One who breaks open the way will go up before them; they will break through the gate and go out. Their king will pass through before them, the LORD at their head" (Micah 2:13 NIV).

"The breaker goes up before them; They break out, pass through the gate and go out by it. So their king goes on before them, And the LORD at their head" (Micah 2:13 NASU).

"The breaker is come up before them: they have broken up, and have passed through the gate, and are gone out by it: and their king shall pass before them, and the LORD on the head of them" (Micah 2:13 KJV).

1. *"Let God arise; Let His enemies be scattered"* (Ps. 68:1 NKJV). Let the trumpet sound and heaven's culture come to earth. Let the King of Glory arise that all may know that there is only one true and faithful God—the Lord Almighty...*the One who was and is and is to come* (Rev. 1:8 paraphrased).

2. **You** are the maker of heaven and earth. **You** are the one that finds good pleasure in all that *seek first the Kingdom of God*. So, that is what we do. We seek You with our whole heart...our whole mind...our whole soul and being. Let it be a pleasing aroma to You—the One who sits upon the throne. Let it capture Your heart and attention. Let it release the anointing that breaks through and stops the delay.

3. We cry out, "Come as the Breaker—release the break-through. Come as One who crashes demonic walls, breaks through the enemy's gate, removes Satan's obstacles and crushes every force that stands in Your way!"

4. Wanting Your timing and alignment, we declare, "Your will...not our will be done." We stand ready to be a vessel that You can flow

through to others. We pray for all walls around our hearts to be removed, in the name of Jesus. This allows Your presence to overwhelm every obstruction. We're asking, "Would You surround our hearts with Your hands so that we never close You and others out due to hurt and pain? Would You envelop it so that this is no longer an option?" Our goal is an unencumbered heart—free to hear and see You more clearly; it allows us to flow with You, and our heart to beat in sync with the Lover of our soul—our Bridegroom.

5. This breaker anointing allows us to see the captives set free and alignment take place everywhere the Lord calls us to go and to everyone He calls us to comfort with prayer, deliverance, and ministry. It is not us; it is the Holy Spirit within. We're a vessel who has said, "Yes." This aligns us with heaven, releasing God to flow through us. This makes us shout, sing, dance, proclaim, and pray about the glorious excellency of our God.

6. Our prayers go forth, "Let none stand in the way of Your will being done; let the forces that may trample the majesty of our King be thwarted; let those who oppose step aside so that the King of Glory may come in, sup with us, and God's will be further established today." No going back. "Advance...advance...advance" is our cry.

7. Do not allow the dawdling of our souls to slow us down or impede the forward momentum. We speak to our souls, commanding them to get serious and not allow distractions to be a hindrance. "Our God is an awesome God" sings forth from our mouths as Your ways are established in us, our families, (name your church) _____, this area, and nation.

8. Our heart longs and cries out for the breaker anointing that leads to break-through, alignment, and freedom. We trust You for a magnitude that results in changed lives, sold out to You one hundred percent, leading to revival. It must be in Your time, revival that lasts and transforms an area that affects a nation. Why not, Lord? Use us...use us...use us...that's our plea; that's our prayer; that's our purpose in life.

9. We bind up delay and declare, "We will not stop until the Lord says, *'Well done My good and faithful servants* (Matt. 25:21 paraphrased). *Enter into your rest'*" (Matt. 25:34 paraphrased). Then, we will know that we know. You have heard us, and destiny has been fulfilled. This

is our cry from the depths of our being, in the mighty name of Jesus. Amen!

Twenty-five
Releasing the More

Dedicated to Sondra Gaddy

"Blessed are those who hunger and thirst for righteousness, for they will be filled" (Matt. 5:6 NIV).

1. *"We are not satisfied, Lord! Hear our cry today for 'MORE'! There has to be more and we must have it!"* This is our heart-felt cry from all our yesterdays, today, and until our plea breaks through to heaven.

   We will P-U-S-H:

   <u>P</u>ray <u>U</u>ntil <u>S</u>omething <u>H</u>appens!

   When will it fully ascend and arrive at the throne room of God? Will it reach the ears of the One for whom our hearts longs?

2. We will not give up until it does, and we participate in *the more* in the land of the living with all our being. Until then, allow our longing to become insatiable. Allow the desperation of our hearts and souls to be such that it releases action on our part—not only a crying out night and day...day and night, until You release MORE into the earth, but also until it becomes our reality—our way of life.

3. May this prayer open heaven's gate and release angelic activity to do what we've dreamed about, but have been unable to obtain. We are thirsty; we are hungry. But it's not a natural thirst or hunger. It is supernatural and can only be quenched by You, Jesus, King of Kings and Lord of Lords. You are the One for whom our hearts long. You are the One whom we long to please. So daily we seek Your face and pursue You.

4. We are reminded of a scripture written so long ago, but a word in season for us *today*. *"But when he, the Spirit of truth, comes, he will guide you into all truth. He will not speak on his own; he will speak only what he hears, and he will tell you what is yet to come. He will bring glory to me by taking from what is mine and making it known to you. All that belongs to the Father is mine. That is why I said the Spirit*

will take from what is mine and make it known to you" (John 16:13-15 NIV).

5. "Yes, Lord, yes. Teach us, Lord, to work alongside the Holy Spirit, as He guides us into all truth. Teach us to tap into what You're doing and bring heaven to earth. We are Your vessel. Use us to bring glory to You. Help us, we pray. Help us; we need Your help!"

6. We are also reminded that You spoke of *GREATER… "I tell you the truth, anyone who has faith in me will do what I have been doing. He will do even greater things than these, because I am going to the Father. And I will do whatever you ask in my name, so that the Son may bring glory to the Father. You may ask me for anything in my name, and I will do it"* (John 14:12-14 NIV).

7. Lord, You know what's in our hearts. You put it there. Our hearts burn for the *greater*. This longing keeps us awake at night. Our plea is for You to use us. We're no longer interested in being by-standers. We must see, taste, feel, and experience *the more*. This hooks us into *the greater*. (We're pleading for this in Your name…)

8. This increases our yearning to be holy—a vessel You desire to flow through. We crave to be at Your side, an extension of You in this world to the lost and dying, to those who need salvation, prayer, healing, prophetic ministry, and deliverance. We know it's not only at hand, but it's available in the here and now. We long to step into it every moment of every day.

9. We believe, declare, and profess, "Wherever we go, things change and shift because of *the more* and *greater* anointing that resides in us, on us, and around us." It's the kingdom of God being advanced through us. We declare to our natural man, "Laziness, pride, unforgiveness, anger, disobedience, and fear must go." We no longer allow these to reside in our temple; there is no room for them or lackadaisical, self-promoting attitudes. We establish singleness of mind and spirit. The focus is You.

10. *The more* is here for us. We must step into it. *It's out with the old; in with the new.* We stand in awe of You and say, "Thank You." Those words seem so hollow and we wonder, who are we that You would be mindful of us? The answer is simple. We are King's kids. He heard our cries for *more,* and we will never be the same! What an awesome

God we serve. *"We won't let You down."* That's our declaration, and it's in Your mighty name, Jesus, we pray. Amen.

Twenty-six
Overcoming the Lust of the Flesh
and the Pride of Life

Dedicated to Darleen Lindley

"Love not the world, neither the things that are in the world. If any man love the world, the love of the Father is not in him. For all that is in the world, the lust of the flesh, and the lust of the eyes, and the pride of life, is not of the Father, but is of the world" (1 John 2:15-16 KJV).

"But he said to me, 'My grace is sufficient for you, for my power is made perfect in weakness.' Therefore, I will boast all the more gladly about my weaknesses, so that Christ's power may rest on me. That is why, for Christ's sake, I delight in weaknesses, in insults, in hardships, in persecutions, in difficulties. For when I am weak, then I am strong" (2 Corinthians 12:9-10 NIV).

1. Father, we come in the name of Jesus to confess that we are sinners, saved by grace. The enemy would like us to forget about the saving grace of the cross and keep us in a place of constant turmoil with little or no visible growth. Yet, this grace catapults us to be what and who You declare we are in every situation. It is not grace to do **whatever** we feel like doing; it is grace to go higher and deeper in You…to depart from our natural inclinations and to walk with You as we go through life.

2. We declare today, "We are Your children." The enemy may assail us, knowing our weaknesses. But Your strength keeps us and stabilizes us. It holds us and adjusts us when we need it most. Therefore, I boast in You and You alone. *For you created my inmost being; you knit me together in my mother's womb. I praise you because I am fearfully and wonderfully made; your works are wonderful, I know that full well* (Ps. 139:13–14 NIV).

3. Yet, we gaze upon the invisible shortcomings of our inmost being that stands out to us, which we (wrongly) imagine the world sees. This works to magnify our need for You. Even though we believe that we

are *"fearfully and wonderfully made"* (Ps. 139:14 NIV) *and also the "righteousness of God"* (2 Cor. 5:21 NIV) in Christ Jesus, we cry, *"Help our unbelief!"* (Mark 9:24 paraphrased) This opens our eyes to only one possible conclusion: our need for You is great.

4. In our minds, we understand that You hold first place and are the Lover of our Souls. You are our Bridegroom and soon-coming King. We are Your bride. Then, why do our thoughts and actions betray what we know to be true? Why do we so easily abandon our First Love? Knowing this, we call upon Your name. You bring comfort, joy, hope, grace, healing, love, and peace.

5. You help us make right choices *to do the next right thing.* You remind us of our righteous standing, purchased with Your blood. You remain our hope! We know the plans of the enemy. He comes to *rob, steal, kill, and destroy* (1John 10:10 paraphrased). It plays out in many ways: often as *lust of the flesh, lust of the eyes, and the pride of life* (1John 2:16 paraphrased). Lust—*a powerful force that produces an intense wanting for an object or circumstance fulfilling the soul...* **but** for a moment! In the end, we are left empty, ashamed, and feeling guilty.

6. We declare, *"We are Christians"*—a little Christ. Those things that produce an ungodly lust will never fill the void that can only be filled by YOU. If we hesitate for a moment, it sweeps in with its pledge of desires fulfilled—but gives only empty, hollow, shallow promises...causing this unwanted appetite to overtake us. We know *our spirit is willing* to do what is right, *but our flesh is weak* (Mark 14:38).

7. So today, amid every ungodly ambition that wants to allure and captivate us with its enticing ways, we shout loudly to the King of Kings, repeating the promises that bring life, *"Your grace is sufficient for us, for Your power is made perfect in our weaknesses!"* (2Cor. 12:9 paraphrased). We speak to our flesh and command it to align with Your word once again.

8. We breathe in Your promises. They get through to our hearts and once again bring us the peace that we need for this moment in time. Every breath we breathe is for You. We continue to pray, seek, ask, declare, and yield ourselves to the One who turns our weaknesses into worship and our slip-ups into strength! This is all for Your glory, honor and praise, in Jesus' name. Amen!

Twenty-seven
Jesus has Overcome the World

Dedicated to Noreen Holcomb

"I have told you these things, so that in me you may have peace. In this world you will have trouble. But take heart! I have overcome the world" *(John 16:33 NIV).*

"In this you greatly rejoice, though now for a little while you may have had to suffer grief in all kinds of trials. These have come so that your faith — of greater worth than gold, which perishes even though refined by fire — may be proved genuine and may result in praise, glory and honor when Jesus Christ is revealed" (1 Peter 1:6-7 NIV).

1. *"The name of the Lord is a strong tower; the righteous run in and they are safe"* (Pr. 18:10 NIV). This scripture song goes over and over in our minds and causes us to run into Your arms of love, reminding us there is only ONE who can save (save, heal, and deliver) to the uttermost. You alone are <u>OUR</u> strong tower—able to help us in times of need and suffering.

2. During trials and tribulation, we declare Your word: *You turn my mourning into dancing* (Ps. 30:22 KJV). It's a mystery; we don't know how You do it. Yet we don't look for an explanation. We simply trust You and thank You for hiding us in the shadow of Your wings. During seasons of suffering, we have learned to *surrender all* to You. "Take from us everything that is not worthy of YOU," we pray. "Allow what delights **You** to come forth from us during these times as sweet smelling incense. Take us and mold us. Shape us into Your image. *We are Yours; we are Yours,"* is the cry that comes forth from our lips.

3. When trials and temptations result in pain, torment, and affliction, we long to touch You and experience the beauty of Your holiness, gaze upon Your loveliness, and taste Your amazing grace. Our plea resounds, "Don't let the heavens be as brass, preventing our prayers from ascending to the throne room of God." We repent and forgive quickly so our prayers are unhindered.

4. Who is like You? The answer is simple, yet more complex than our thoughts can fathom or understand. Even so, *we know that we know* that Your love is abundantly available to us. In a moment of time beyond our comprehension, You allow us to tangibly assimilate this into our spirit-man and at the same time forbid the enemy to take us captive or release unspeakable condemnation upon us. We remain secure and invisible from him...in a hidden place, under the shadow of Your wings (Ps. 91:4 paraphrased).

5. We will not give up until we see You move on our behalf in the land of the living. Though our bodies may be frail; our spirits soar on wings of eagles and we release this prayer. "Help us O Lord; *our spirit is willing; but our flesh is weak*" (Mark 14: 38 paraphrased). We hear You clearly, "Don't allow any suffering to be wasted; allow it to have its perfect way so that eternal purposes may be worked out."

6. During this, we know You are refining us like gold. You remind us that You have not only overcome the world, but have brought us peace—even when troubles, trials, and sufferings come our way as a part of life. But You never give up on us, and this makes us smile. We are sure our *faith is being proved genuine and **will** result in praise, glory and honor when Jesus Christ is revealed* (1Pt. 5:7 paraphrased). How can this be? We don't know, yet we love to meditate on it...Your will be done in the mighty name of Jesus. Amen!

Twenty-eight
Come up Higher, My Beloved

Dedicated to the Mountain Movers Prayer Group

"My beloved is mine, and I am his..." (Song of Sol. 2:16 KJV).

"Can you fathom the mysteries of God? Can you probe the limits of the Almighty? They are higher than the heavens — what can you do? They are deeper than the depths of the grave — what can you know?" (Job 11:7-8 NIV).

"He who descended is the very one who ascended higher than all the heavens..." (Eph. 4:10 NIV).

The following is a prophetic word from the Lord, given to me for the Mountain Movers Prophetic Prayer Group, upon which this prayer is based. Please note, to the best of my ability, the wording and grammar is exactly as spoken to me by the Lord.

> *"God is seated on the throne...higher than any—more than your imagination can take you...farther than the eye can see. Eye has not seen nor has ear heard that which God has planned for His beloved—His bride. It is a time of going higher and deeper—wider and farther. Who can fathom the unfathomable? Who can understand the ways of our King? His love is unlimited; His ways are boundless without measure. This uncreated, indescribable, un-comprehensible God has come and involves you in His affairs. He bids you, 'Come up higher, my beloved. Come up where I take your breath away. Breathe in Me and I will show you things that not many have ever tempted to know or see. Come up higher my beloved.'"*

1. Heavenly Father, we come to You in the mighty name of Jesus, undone by this one thought, "We are Your beloved; You are ours, and You bid us to 'come higher'." How awesome are Your thoughts and

ways toward us. How incredible it is to come into Your presence. We do so with thanksgiving and praise. We worship and adore You, the One True Living God. There is none like You.

2. Your presence permeates our thoughts, ways, and being. We declare from every fiber of our being, with all that we are, "You are ours, and we are Yours!" There is none like You. We want to see You…to know You…to hear You—today and every day, in the land of the living. We want to go higher and deeper in You. We long to experience the vastness of Your presence. What does this look like, feel like… to know that which is incomprehensible? Allow us for a moment to gaze upon Your loveliness and sense Your goodness and grace. It is too magnificent for words. How we long for You.

3. Our heart beats fast at this mere thought. The One who calls me to come higher is the King of Kings and Lord of Lords. Your love for us is more than we can handle, and can't be understood in just one lifetime. Your delight for us, mere mortals, leaves us undone and shaking our heads. We stand in awe of You. We are overwhelmed—a lovesick child who has eyes only for You—our Bridegroom.

4. We try to fathom what all this means, but it is impossible. We know that *when we see You, we will be like You* (1John 3:2 paraphrased). We long for that day, and at the same time we tremble at the mere thought of it. We want to go deeper with You. Will You help us? Will You teach us? Will You lead us? We want to be in sync with You. Each beat of Your heart; each step You take, we want to align with You, observing the blueprint You have for us and walking it out with You, bringing heaven to earth…every step…every breath…every moment of every day!

5. Is this even possible? Is destiny even within our reach? We believe it is. We pray it, declare it, decree it, receive it, and walk in it. Your plan… Your will... Your angels released on our behalf so we can perform the very thing that we were created for, and that which You placed in our hearts to do and be. We are part of the Esther generation, and we live *for such a time as this* (Esther 4:14 paraphrased). Do not shield us from what lies ahead; we are Your design, and all that You created *is good* (Gen. 1:31 paraphrased).

6. These are Your intentions inside of us whispered…spoken, and shouted. Heaven is in our hearts, and we release it to the four corners

of the earth as we pray Your will over us, our families, churches, and this nation. We don't give up or back down. Destiny is within reach. We will not stop or look back. We look forward to the day when You say, *"'Well done,'* (Matt. 25: 23 NIV) *My beloved—My bride; enter into your rest. The best is yet to come."*

7. Our hearts align with this, and we hear You speak, "Fear not; you are in My hands; I will never leave you nor forsake you." (Deut. 31: 6 paraphrased). We trust You and believe it.

8. With just one glance You have left us undone. We come to You; the veil has been rent. We come in because we can. You made the way. It was by Your blood. May we never get used to this fact, and may we never take for granted what Your blood did for us. It is still active and alive. One decision to say, "Yes," has changed the course of our history. *We were bought with a price. We are not our own* (1Cor. 6:20 paraphrased). For this and so much more, we are forever thankful. We give all that we are to You in the mighty name of Jesus. Take us higher. Amen.

Twenty-nine
All In

Dedicated to Michele White, Tina Watson, Jan Colver, and Pamela Hill Tarlton

"Draw near to God and he will draw near to you" (James 4:8 NKJV).

"And whatever you do, whether in word or deed, do it all in the name of the Lord Jesus, giving thanks to God the Father through him" (Col. 3:17 NIV).

1. Holy Spirit, come as our comforter and the one who teaches and guides us into all truth. Forgive us, Lord, for not allowing the Holy Spirit to have His way one hundred percent of the time. Forgive us for thinking more highly of ourselves than we ought. Forgive us for not allowing Your ways to encompass us all the time.

2. We're ***all in*** because You're an ***all-in*** God. We don't want to do this thing termed Christianity halfway or halfheartedly. We don't want to lose sight of You at any time. We want Your ways to be our ways.

3. Let it be such that nobody can see where You start and end and where we start and end. Please, Lord, hear our plea today. We cry out for help! Can You hear us? Will You touch us? Will You teach us? Will You contend for us?

4. Allow Your breath to breathe through every pore of our being. We are desperate for You. We're lost without You. We can fathom no other way of life. We live, eat, and breathe You. We move to the movement of Your thoughts…Your whisper…Your voice. Our goal is YOU—to be in sync with You. Let the waves of Your presence hit us and fill us. We long for You: "More, Lord, more!"

5. Even now, we hear the sounds of heaven as the trumpet signals the announcing and beckoning to us—Your bride. You are calling us to come hither. You've heard our cries of desperation and You're sounding the trumpet, announcing Your decrees for us. (We question, "What does this mean?")

6. Then we hear the breaking of glass. You're breaking off all the false ideas and ideals that have kept us from a true encounter with You—the living and One True God. It is these false ideas and facades that have kept us from getting closer and closer to You and others. (Help us lay them at Your footstool.)

7. Today is the day that we choose to do all in Your name and for Your glory. We declare that breakthrough is coming forth; the breaking of old habits, ways, thinking and ideas. These no longer impede our relationship with You nor the destiny You have set before us. Thank You for the sounds of heaven that are breaking forth to accomplish Your will to bring heaven to earth and shift the atmosphere around us, our families, _____ (name your church and area).

8. This is the day that we choose to draw even nearer than we ever have before. As we draw near to You, You draw near to us. Nothing could be sweeter at this moment in time. Thank You for Your divine presence that inhabits and surrounds us. We stand in awe of You as the sounds of heaven resound around us, for Your glory. In the name of Jesus. Amen.

Thirty
Kisses of Your Lips

Dedicated to Pete Mullins

Let him kiss me with the kisses of his mouth — for your love is more delightful than wine. Pleasing is the fragrance of your perfumes; your name is like perfume poured out. No wonder the maidens love you! Take me away with you — let us hurry! Let the king bring me into his chambers. We rejoice and delight in you; we will praise your love more than wine. How right they are to adore you!" (Song of Songs 1:2-4 NIV).

1. How we long for You today; whether in this extremely dry and thirsty land—or even in the land of plentiful. How we never want to depart from the delight that the mere thought of You brings us. Therefore, we come into agreement with Your word, and we long to taste that which only You can bestow upon us—the kisses of Your lips.

2. What does it taste like, feel like, smell like? What is it that makes Your kisses more delightful than wine, a fragrance like perfume? It is the unknown factor in the equation of life. It is You and You alone…the triune God upon mere human vessels, who comes without words, but with love that emanates through every pore of our beings. It is a closeness that can't be bought or sold. It can only be given by the Holy One of Israel; it can only be received by Your lovesick child that seeks You above all else.

3. Let us be the maiden—the bride, that goes after You with all that we are. We cry out, "Let it be us! Take us with You. Let us hurry away with You to Your chambers. We want to rejoice and delight in You even more than we ever have. We want to praise and love You more and more. We adore You."

4. Let our adoration play out before You, our King, in inexplicable ways. Let our imagination be purified and sanctified by the touch of the Master's hands. Let us be the ones who run with You, receive power from on High, and do mighty exploits with You. Let it be us.

5. We never want to grow weary in well doing, but in all our ways let us seek You first. Then we know You will direct our paths. Let us be the ones who are holy, pleasing, and undefiled—fit for a King. This is our heart; this is our cry: "Let us run together, arm-in-arm, hand-in-hand, never separated—doing those things that You created us to do—those things that can only come about or be realized because we have been kissed by the *kisses of Your mouth*." (Song of Songs 1:2 paraphrased).

6. The breath of God flows in us and through us. It engulfs us and circulates around us like a whirlwind. We are no longer our own; we fulfill, to the fullest capacity, that for which You created us to be and do. We don't stop until our destinies are fulfilled, and we hear You say, "'*Well done good and faithful servant*' (Matt. 25:23 NIV*). You have reached your destiny. 'Enter into your rest.'*"

7. With just one kiss, one breath, and one moment with the King, we are changed forever. Nothing will ever be the same. How we love You more each day. Let us not fail to give of ourselves to You. Allow this holy kiss to cause us to transcend who we are to become who You say we are. How we love You and long for You, our most holy and precious Lord. In Jesus' name we pray. Amen.

It would be a joy and pleasure to hear your testimony from reading this book. If you would like Sharon to minister, please feel free to contact her at **shift.sharon@gmail.com**. She is well equipped and has much experience in ministering in the following broad categories:

- Prayer

- Deliverance

- Prophecy

- Mentoring & leadership